Seasonal Expectations

An Essential Guide to
Gardening, Foods, Festivals & Outings
In the Greater San Francisco Bay Area

Katherine Grace Endicott

Book design: Katherine Housman
Illustrations: Greg Rogers and Andrea Hendrick
Type design book cover: Dave Mentzer and Andrea Hendrick
Editing: Linda Nicholson and Nora Harlow
This book was set in ITC New Baskerville with Xerox Ventura Publisher™ by
Ocean View Technical Publications

Library of Congress Cataloging in Publication Data

Endicott, Katherine Grace.
    Seasonal expectations.

    Includes index.
    1. San Francisco Bay Area (Calif.)—Description and travel—Guide-books.
2. Gardening—California—San Francisco Bay Area.   3. Cookery.   4. Food.
5. Festivals—California—San Francisco Bay Area.
I. Title.
R868.S156E5   917.94'60453   84-71853
ISBN 0-935382-72-0

Printed in the U.S.A.

Tioga Publishing Company
Box 50490
Palo Alto, CA 94303

To my sister Carolyn

To everything there is a season, and a time to every purpose under the heaven.
Ecclesiastes, 3:1

Preface

As I scurry and worry my way through daily tasks great winds hurl clouds overhead. This book was written to open the door to my well-insulated, artificially lighted house and yell, "Hey look at those clouds." It was written because I want to experience the seasonal pleasure of the passing months, and to feel connected to the natural rhythms of the greater San Francisco Bay Area.

The book is divided into sections reflecting the five Bay Area seasons that influence our attitudes as well as our wardrobes. The seasons are defined at the beginning of each section. Within each section the months are divided into the pleasures closely connected to the seasons: gardening, foods, celebrations, and outings. This is a highly personal book—one woman's opinion on how to savor each month's seasonal pleasures.

This is also a practical book. "Sentimentality," wrote James Baldwin, "is a spurious emotion." There is no need to persuade anyone of the pleasures of tasting March's first, crisp asparagus sauteed with butter, or the joy of watching a fledgling egret take flight in May, or the thrill of hearing a jazz trumpet wail out into the August night. We only need to be reminded when and where.

No serious Bay Area gardener doubts we have seasons—the year is too clearly divided into seasonal cycles of tasks and pleasures. The gardening section is a monthly list of what to do when, plus special articles to add to your seasonal pleasures such as planting bare-root cane berries in February, or harvesting herbs in September, or sowing wildflower seeds in November to be nurtured by the winter rain.

There is no dull season for cooks in the Bay Area's culinary paradise between vineyards and crop lands. Each month brings new pleasures to anticipate and enjoy. Spring's sweet berries are succeeded by summer's lush vegetables, then by fall's crisp apples and new cheeses, and finally by winter's roasting fowl and rich confections. The food section is a monthly list of what is in season and how to select it.

The celebrations section highlights hundreds of local festivals, giving a brief indication of what to expect. National and religious holidays are also listed and explained. Every month brings a variety of celebrations.

One of the great seasonal pleasures of Bay Area living is the variety of nearby beautiful areas. Many of the outings in this book can be taken throughout the year—they are listed in a month that will enhance the experience. Within a day's drive there are the granite cliffs of Yosemite—especially fine in May when the falls are full; or the turquoise waves and white sands of Carmel—so relaxing in the warm, fogless days of October; or the vineyards of Napa Valley—aromatic during September's grape harvest.

Memorable seasonal outings are also centered around natural phenomena. A February trip to see the elephant seals of Año Nuevo is as compelling as a safari to gaze at wallowing hippopotamuses. March is a good month to view sea otter pups in the kelp beds near Monterey. May is fine for watching the majestic herons and egrets at the Audubon Canyon Ranch. And October and November are the months to view the return migration of the monarch butterfly.

I would also like to thank the many supporters of the first edition of *Seasonal Expectations* such as M.F.K. Fisher, who wrote encouraging words to an unknown writer, Jim Dunbar of KGO radio, whose enthusiasm for Mother Nature made my first radio interview a joy, and the book reviewers and editors who brought this regional book to the attention of California readers.

Updating and revising the second edition has been a pleasure. As the gardening columnist for the *San Francisco Chronicle*, I have become increasingly aware of the importance of growing plants that are well suited to the dry summers and wet winters in Northern California. Therefore, the gardening section has been revised for the 1990s to include more native and drought-resistant plants. Ironically, many California native plants such as the lovely white-flowered *Carpenteria californica* and the wildflower called 'baby blue-eyes' are widely grown in England but are practically unknown here. Native plants that are easy to care for and beautiful to look at have been featured throughout the revised edition.

Finally, I want to thank my husband, Steven Mendelson, for his continued support for this project.

Illustrations

Pacific gray whale: 3
California sea lion: 15
Strawberries: 18
Elephant seals: 24
Harbor seals: 26
Sea otter: 33
Pacific coast iris: 45
Fairy lanterns: 55
Stream violet: 56
Redwood sorrel: 56
Yerba santa: 59
Yarrow: 59
Poppy: 60
Tidy tips: 60
Pelargonium: 63
Red raspberries: 79
Grasshoppers: 91
Aphids: 94
Earwigs: 94
Scales: 94
Hermit crab: 105
Sea anemones: 113
Limpets: 113
Starfish: 114
Mussels: 114
Wine country picnic: 121
Pumpkins: 135

Canada goose: 149
Cormorants: 157
Gulls: 158
Pelican: 158
Coots: 159
Monarch butterfly: 161
Christmas tree farms: 163
Mountain winter: 168

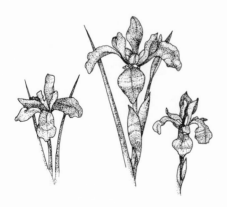

Contents

The Wet Season: 1
  January: 3
  February: 15

The Season of Wind and Fog: 31
  March: 33
  April: 45
  May: 63

The Variable Season: 77
  June: 79
  July: 91
  August: 105

The Indian Summer Season: 119
  September: 121
  October: 135

The Silver Season: 147
  November: 149
  December: 163

Gardening Update: 174

Ready Reference—Gardening: 181
Ready Reference—Foods: 185
Ready Reference—Celebrations & Outings: 188

Recipes

Deep-fried baby artichokes: 7
Preserving berries: 83
Cantaloupe with Cointreau: 97
Watermelon spiked with white wine: 97
Harvesting herbs: 122
Elephant garlic paste: 124
Barbecued Pacific oysters: 124
Bouquet garni: 126
Herb salt: 126
Herb vinegar: 126
Herb compound butter: 126
Mint jelly: 127
Mint tea: 127
Pesto: 127
Basil and mint salad dressing: 127
Fresh pumpkin pie: 139
Roasted pumpkin seeds: 139
Roasted chestnuts: 152
Cranberry sauce: 166

The Wet Season

Temperature—cold
low forties to high fifties

Rain

This is the cold, wet season when the storms pile up one behind another off the coast, and the sky does not clear for days. When storms blow down from Alaska, the air can be icy cold and snow may fall on Mount Tamalpais, Mount Hamilton, and Mount Diablo. The Alaskan storms drop powder snow in the high Sierra Nevada. But if storms blow in from Hawaii, the warm rain turns the ski slopes into soggy mush and the melting snow creates the danger of flooding.

Rainfall varies greatly from San Jose's relatively dry annual 13 inches to San Rafael's heavy annual 35 inches to Boulder Creek's (Santa Cruz Mountains) astonishing annual 60 inches.

Radiation Fog

Radiation fog is another wet season phenomenon. During the cold predawn hours, the airborne moisture from the rain-soaked earth condenses into a fog which hangs in low, damp areas such as the Delta marshes. Tule plants growing in these marshes generate the local name "tule fog." This low, dense fog floats from the valleys into the Bay Area creating a motorist's nightmare and sometimes closing both the Oakland and San Francisco airports.

Gardening

The wet season is not a good one for gardeners. The ground is usually too soaked to be properly spaded. And gardeners must watch for the cold, clear nights threatening frost. But it is a season for bare-root planting, pruning, and armchair browsing through garden catalogs.

Outings

When it rains hard, the Japan Center Complex in Sam Francisco offers interesting sheltered arcades and underground parking. If rain only threatens, in the city's Chinatown is full of colorful stores and warm dim sum restaurants to dash into during a deluge. Two or three times during the season, dry, cold polar air sweeps into the Bay Area bringing sparkling clear weather. This is a perfect time to bundle up and scan the coast for migrating gray whales or drive to Año Nuevo to see the elephant seals.

Seasonal Reminders

In addition to the outings recommended for January and February, the following phenomenon provides an alternative seasonal excursion.

Monarch Butterflies

Monarch butterflies form hanging clusters in Pacific Grove and at Natural Bridges State Beach in Santa Cruz. See November outings page 161. They may be observed through February.

January

Pacific Gray Whale—California State Mammal

January Gardening

In Bloom

Annuals: calendula, Iceland poppy, and pansy
Perennials: cineraria, cyclamen, primrose, and violet
Shrubs: azalea, camellia, and poinsettia
Bulb-like: calla and early blooming narcissus

Holiday gift plants—such as azalea, cyclamen, poinsettia and chrysanthemum—should be moved outdoors when the flowers fade.

Begin planting gladiolus corms this month. Plant gladiolus corms every two or three weeks through April to produce a succession of blooms throughout the summer.

Pick up fallen camellia flowers to help prevent the spread of camellia petal blight.

January is the last month to sow seeds for cool season crops: beets, broccoli, carrots, chard, lettuce, onions, peas, spinach, and turnips.

Prune

Prune deciduous dormant plants, such as fruit trees, roses, grapes, and cane berries, as their buds begin to swell.

In pruning roses, remember that they bloom only on new wood, so you want to promote as much healthy new wood as possible. Generally, roses should be cut back one-third to one-half leaving canes at least 18 inches long. Cut above a swelling bud pointing out from the center. Remove all suckers and dead wood.

Frost Protection

Protect tender plants against frost. January typically is the frostiest month of the year. When the temperature drops toward freezing, move container-grown plants under the eave of an overhanging roof or beneath a leafy tree. Cover plants that are open to the sky by setting stakes in the ground and draping burlap, plastic, old drapes, sheets, or newspaper over the stakes. Make certain the covering does not touch the plant. Cardboard boxes also make good nighttime covers. Remember to remove the covering the next morning when the temperature rises. You can also wrap the trunks of young, tender citrus trees in burlap or paper. Bougainvillea, citrus, fuchsias, and succulents are some plants that need protection.

In the Nursery Look for:

Bare-root roses
Deciduous fruit, nut, and shade trees
Cane berries, strawberries, and grapes
Bare-root vines: clematis and wisteria
Bare-root deciduous shrubs: forsythia, lilac, and rose of Sharon

January is a great month to buy bare-root plants which are dug up while dormant and sold more cheaply than container-grown plants. Look for well-developed, knot-free roots; smooth, unblemished bark; plump buds; and a healthy, well-branched top. If your garden soil is too wet and heavy for planting, cover the roots with damp soil for later planting.

Bare-root Roses

The following roses are favorites of members of rose societies in the San Francisco Bay region—hybrid teas: "Duet," "Granada," "Mister Lincoln," "Pascali," and "Peace"; floribundas: "Cherish" and "Iceberg; grandifloras: "Aquarius," "Gold Metal," and "Queen Elizabeth." Local consulting rosarians offer free rose-growing advice—find them by writing the American Rose Society at P.O. Box 30,000, Shreveport, LA 71130.

Bare-root Vegetables

Plant bare-root perennial vegetables such as artichokes, a large plant 6 feet high, and 6 to 8 feet wide when fully grown; asparagus, planted in well-prepared trenches (its delicate, airy top-growth is often mistaken for a fern); rhubarb; and horseradish. For buying and planting bare-root raspberries, strawberries, and blackberries, see the February gardening section.

Dormant Spray

Spray fruit trees and roses with a dormant spray. Copper oil, or lime-sulfur and oil sprays are considered safe. They are nonpoisonous and do not threaten your garden's ecosystem. Dormant sprays kill aphids, red spiders, mealy bugs, fungus spores, and scale insects—that lay eggs on tree bark. Before spraying, shake off any diseased leaves and rake up and remove dead and fallen leaves. Then drench trunks, branches, and stems with dormant spray. Do not let the spray drift over to any nearby evergreens.

January Foods

Exotic Citrus

January is a great month for exotic citrus. The tangelo, a cross between tangerine and grapefruit, is sweet and tangy. Varieties include 'Minneola' (considered superior), 'Orlando' and 'Sampson.' The tangor, a cross between tangerine and orange, is a large, easy-to-peel, sweet fruit—the best known variety is 'Temple.' 'Lavender Gem,' a cross between a mandarin and grapefruit, is distinctively colored—a yellow skin with pink flesh. The blood orange, with sweet, red pulp, is often used for juice. The bitter taste of the Seville orange makes it perfect for marmalade or a sauce for duck.

Winter Salad Greens

Some of the most flavorful salad greens are sold in January.

Field lettuce (also called lamb's tongue because of its tongue-shaped leaf) is a memorable green which deserves a delicate dressing.

Romaine is a crisp distinctive lettuce which is assertive enough for a robust dressing.

Watercress, with its sharp, almost bitter taste, makes a choice salad, but it must be used promptly as it may turn an unattractive yellow when refrigerated several days.

Escarole is a close relative of Belgian endive and curly endive. It has a slightly bitter taste. Escarole is excellent as a salad green but it can also be used in soups or braised with butter.

Shellfish

January is an excellent month to buy shellfish such as Pacific spiny lobster, Dungeness crab, Pacific oysters, and clams. Because clams and mussels are considered tastier in the colder winter months, January is a good month to make cioppino—San Francisco's hearty fish soup.

Herring

Pacific herring spawn in Richardson's Bay—roughly located between Sausalito and Tiburon—in January or February. The season is brief but lucrative for fishermen. Most is sent out of the states—the Japanese pay high prices for herring roe. During the season both Pacific herring and herring roe are available in some Bay Area fish markets. Herring is good pickled, baked, or grilled. Herring roe may be cured in a brine solution like caviar.

Cardoon

The cardoon is a vegetable that resembles a mammoth celery. Like the artichoke it is a member of the thistle family—unlike the artichoke, the root and tender interior stalks are edible. The flavor of a cardoon is a mixture of celery and artichoke flavors. The outer stalks of a cardoon are usually discarded—the tender interior stalks and heart are simmered in soup, or braised and served as a vegetable side dish. Cardoons are relatively tough—lengthy simmering or braising is required to tenderize them. Cardoons are available in some produce markets, particularly Italian markets.

Artichoke

Although an expensive delicacy elsewhere, in our culinary paradise the green globe artichoke is everyday fare. Artichokes are grown near Castroville not far from Monterey. When buying an artichoke, look for a compact, green head and tightly closed leaves. Avoid an artichoke with petals that have started to open or with a grayish cast, which indicates toughness. The smaller the artichoke the more tender the leaves and the bottom.

Deep-Fried Baby Artichokes

Baby artichokes are so uncommon outside of the Bay Area, few cookbooks include recipes for them. Locally, gourmet produce markets sell baby artichokes—supermarkets occasionally carry them. The following recipe can be used either as an hors d'oeuvre or as a vegetable side dish.

12 tiny artichokes	¼ teaspoon ground paprika
1 egg, beaten	¼ teaspoon dry mustard
⅓ cup of beer	1 teaspoon double-acting baking
½ teaspoon salt	powder
Oil for deep-frying	¾ cup flour
⅓ cup freshly grated Parmesan cheese	

Wash; cut off prickly tops; and split each baby artichoke in half. Mix egg, beer, salt, paprika, baking powder, and mustard until frothy; then add flour, stirring well. Dip the artichokes into the batter and deep-fry in the oil heated to 375 °F. Turn once and remove when brown. Drain on paper towels. Sprinkle with Parmesan cheese and serve with lemon wedges.

January Celebrations

An Introduction to Celebrations

Unlike gardening, foods, and outings that are usually individual responses to seasonal changes, celebrations are man-made events meant to be shared. From holidays to holy days, seasonal celebrations are a way of joining with others for a common purpose. They bring joy and meaning to our calendar days.

Many celebrations are closely tied to the season. Dog-sled races and winter carnivals are dependent upon snow. Spring fairs and the opening day of the yachting season celebrate the weather's transition from one season to the next. Other celebrations, such as garlic festivals, grape festivals, and pumpkin festivals, are dependent upon seasonal harvests.

Some celebrations, such as Easter, have been observed for nearly 2,000 years. Others, May Day, for instance, draw upon even older rites, such as the pagan rites of spring. As the basis for both nostalgia and anticipation, seasonal celebrations can give continuity to our lives from year to year and from generation to generation.

Specific dates for many local celebrations are not given in this book because they change frequently. The Ready Reference—Celebrations and Outings (under individual headings) lists telephone numbers where current information on each event can be obtained.

Federal and Legal Holidays

New Year's Day—January 1
Washington's Birthday—February 22, observed the third Monday in February
Memorial Day—May 30, observed the last Monday in May
Independence Day—July 4
Labor Day—First Monday in September
Columbus Day—October 12, observed the second Monday in October
Veterans Day—November 11
Thanksgiving—Always the fourth Thursday in November
Christmas—December 25

Additional California Holidays

Martin Luther King Jr. Day—January 15
Lincoln's Birthday—February 12, observed the third Monday in February
Admission Day—September 9

January Celebrations

Because January is usually cold and rainy very few seasonal celebrations are held this month. Gardeners are not encouraged by the dismal weather; nonetheless, it is time to prune roses, and several local rose societies give demonstrations of rose pruning this month. In Oakland, members of the Rose Garden staff and the East Bay Rose Society give demonstrations at the Morcom Amphitheater of Roses. In San Francisco, members of the San Francisco Rose Society give demonstrations in the Rose Garden at Golden Gate Park.

McCloud Dog Sled Races—McCloud

Of course, one way to beat the January rainy-weather blues is to head for the snow. The McCloud Dog Sled Races are some of the largest in the West. The races are sponsored by the quaint, turn-of-the-century town of McCloud, which is located near Mt. Shasta.

Mushroom Fair—Coyote Point

This two-day event begins on Saturday when mycologists lead public forays in search of local edible mushrooms such as the *Clitocybe nuda*—a purple fungus found under oak trees. Participants should come equipped with deep baskets, knives, and wax paper. The mushroom fair at the Coyote Point Museum, located in San Mateo, is held on a Sunday. Preregister by phoning the museum.

Old Time Fiddlers Contest—Cloverdale

The small argricultural community of Cloverdale, located on Highway 101 between Santa Rosa and Ukiah, is the site of the annual Old Time Fiddlers Contest and Show. Sponsored by the local Historical Society, the contest and show are held at the Citrus Fairgrounds.

Chinese New Year

Chinese New Year usually is in February. Please see page 22.

Remember the day, even the month of an event may change from year to year. For more information see the Ready Reference—Celebrations & Outings (under individual headings).

January Outings

Pacific Gray Whale

The whalebone or baleen whales are the largest animals that have ever lived. The Pacific gray whale (illustrated on the January cover page) can reach a length of 50 feet. The largest whalebone whale is the female blue whale which can reach 100 feet long and weigh 150 tons!

Whalebone whales are named for a long horny plate of baleen attached to the roof of their mouths—the inner edge and tip of the baleen plate are frayed into long, hair-like bristles which serve as a filter to trap minute forms of sea life from sea water. Baleen is a tough and elastic substance similar to claws, fingernails, and cattle horns. Baleen, also known as whalebone, was used to stiffen corsets and collars in the 1800s. Despite their mammoth size and the mind-boggling quantity of sea water they filter, their throats are no larger in diameter than a man's fist.

During the summer months gray whales live in the Bering Sea (Arctic water between Russia and Alaska) where they feed on krill (small crustaceans). During the fall and early winter they migrate south—the females are impregnated on this journey. Calves conceived the year before are born in Baja California—the gestation period is thirteen months. At Baja California the whales feed on sardines and anchovies. By March the gray whales begin their migration north.

When to Watch

January is the best month for whale watching, and March the second best. From November through January (with stragglers in February), approximately 1700 gray whales migrate from the Bering Sea to Baja California. They return from March through April.

What to Look for

Remember to bring binoculars. Gray whales keep close to shallow, coastal waters. They are often spotted by the spume of water they exhale when they dive. After sounding (diving) for 8 to 10 minutes, the gray whale sends up a spout of water 10 to 12 feet high. It is impossible to predict where they will surface—maybe they will surface in the same place or 1,000 feet further along. Sometimes gray whales flap their flukes (tails) and once in a while they breach (jump) almost entirely out of the water. It is possible to see a gray whale any month of the year. Some get lazy about migrating and just hang around.

Where to Watch

Point Reyes Lighthouse is the best place for shore watching. The Point Reyes Lighthouse is situated in Point Reyes National Seashore on the blunt headland that juts far out into the Pacific Ocean—the headland offers a superior vantage point.

Located 50 miles north of the Bay Area via Highway 1 and Sir Frances Drake Boulevard, Point Reyes National Seashore is a diverse area of forest, dunes, and beaches (see September outings). The Visitor's Center on Drake's Beach often runs weekend whale-watching shuttle buses out to the lighthouse.

Once you reach the lighthouse at the end of Sir Frances Drake Boulevard, it is a brisk ten-minute walk from the parking lot to the cliffs where many people prefer to whale-watch.

Davenport is another fine whale-watching area. From the parking lot of Whale Watchers Bluff you can spot whales during the migration. The small town of Davenport is located 11 miles north of Santa Cruz on Highway 1. In the 1800s Davenport was a whaling town. There was a large whaling station in nearby Moss Landing. (There was even a whaling station in San Francisco.) In 1971 the United States Department of Commerce banned commercial whaling by United States vessels.

Other observation areas include Fort Ross, Patrick Point, Pigeon Point, Point Lobos, Point Loma, Point Sur, and Salt Point. All these areas offer vantage points suitable for whale watching.

Whale Watching Expeditions

For closer observation, there are two- to eight-hour whale observation boat trips, and boat trips lasting up to seven days. It is possible to see many different whales in the Bay Area, including blue, killer, and humpback whales. The Oceanic Society and the national headquarters of the Whale Center offer trips with guides during most of the year. From January through March, sport-fishing operators offer short (about two hours) observation trips out of Monterey and other coastal areas. The Oceanic Society recommends bringing a raincoat and taking a motion-sickness medication before departure.

For more information on whale trips, whale observation areas, and whale exhibits consult the Ready Reference—Celebrations & Outings (Pacific gray whale).

January Outings

San Francisco's Chinatown

Chinatown, at the approach of Chinese New Year (usually celebrated in February), is a perfect excursion when January's unsympathetic weather makes longer journeys unappealing.

Walking Tour of Chinatown

A convenient place to begin a walking tour of Chinatown is at the ornate gateway—with its sculptured lions—where Grant Avenue meets Bush Street. Walk up Grant Avenue noticing the fascinating Chinese art and antique shops. Look for fine rosewood copies of Ming dynasty furniture, intricate cloisonne, and beautiful porcelains. This is also a good area for Chinese clothing, such as silk jackets and embroidered pajamas. Many Grant Avenue stores remain open until 10 P.M.

When you reach Sacramento Street, turn left and walk uphill one block and then right onto Waverly Place—also known as the Street of the Painted Balconies. At 119 Waverly is the headquarters of Chinatown's most popular newspaper, the *Chinese Times*. Look for the newspaper in the window. Waverly Place is also the location of several Chinese benevolent associations and Chinese temples. The temples are small and the visiting hours unpredictable. One of the oldest, dating from the Gold Rush era, is the *T'ien Hou* Temple on the fourth floor at 125 Waverly. If you look up at this brightly painted building and see blue incense smoke swirling from the fourth floor balcony, it is probably open. Inside the small sanctuary there are intricately carved statues. To reach the temple climb the stairs—there is no elevator.

Waverly Place dead ends on Washington Street—where you should look for the Tai Fung Wo & Co., at 857 Washington. This old herb company sells tiger bones, dried sea horses, scorpions, and centipedes. Down the street at 812 Washington is the Mee On Co., a Chinese candy store selling a wide variety of dried and candied fruit, such as ginger, coconut, melon, pineapple, lotus, and plum. The plums come in several concentrations of sweet, sour, or salty. Eat them by sucking on the meaty, brown coated seed until the flavor is gone.

Walk up Washington Street and right on Ross Alley (once an area of opium dens and downstairs gambling houses) to Jackson. Walk up Jackson to Stockton. On weekends this area is a huge open-air market. In preparation for Chinese New Year, red-flowered azaleas and anthuriums are sold to bring the recipient good luck in the coming year.

Dining on Dim Sum

One block to the right on Stockton Street is Pacific Street where several large tea houses are located. The Ready Reference—Celebrations and Outings (Chinatown) lists several nearby tea houses. San Francisco's Chinatown is one of the few cities with tea houses offering the wonderful, tasty delicacies known as *dim sum*. San Francisco tea houses are generally open from 9 A.M. to 3 P.M.

Begin by ordering a tea, such as a full-bodied, fermented black tea (actually copper red); a semi-fermented *oolong*; a less fermented *pouchong* (scented with jasmine and gardenia); or a green tea—jasmine or chrysanthemum. Beer also goes well with dim sum.

When a waitress passes with a tray or cart, motion to her and point to what looks good. More trays will offer different tiny dishes of spring rolls, fried pastries, won ton covered meat balls, meat-filled steamed dumplings, shrimp turnovers, pot stickers, pork buns, chicken legs, duck's feet, and other savory items. There also will be a tray of dessert items, such as sliced melon, pale white almond custard with canned fruit, and yellow custard tarts. The waitress will count the number of dishes on your table to determine your bill.

Concluding the Walking Tour

After eating, continue down Pacific Street and turn right on Grant Avenue where markets brim with cages of live poultry and tanks of swimming fish. Chinatown markets have special permission to sell live fowl—the Chinese like their poultry and fish truly fresh. Incidentally, the roast Peking-style duck hanging up for sale is excellent—the skin crisp and the meat succulent.

When you reach Washington Street turn downhill one short block to Breham Place which borders Portsmouth Square—one of the oldest squares in San Francisco. Continue on Breham Place to Clay Street then downhill one-half block and right on Kearny Street one block—then turn right on the interesting, brick-paved Commercial Street. Before leaving Chinatown you might want to visit one of the Chinese bakeries and take home a selection of fried pastry bow ties, moon cakes filled with bean paste, or diamond-shaped sweet rice cakes. A left on Grant Avenue leads to the Chinatown Gate.

For more information see the Ready Reference—Celebrations & Outings under (Chinatown).

January Outings

Sausalito

Sausalito is one of the Bay Area's most charming sea-front towns—not a historically preserved Portofino, but definitely a village by the sea. Sausalito's history is almost as old as San Francisco's. It becomes a true fishing village in January, when the herring run.

The Herring

The Pacific herring migrate to Richardson Bay to spawn sometime between early January and mid-February. For a few days or weeks—depending upon how fast the fishing quota is filled—the bay off of Sausalito is thick with net-casting commercial fishermen. The bay water is churned by feasting harbor seals and the sky is clouded with hungry gulls and pelicans—all of them are after the herring. The smell . . . well the smell is briny.

The problem with viewing all of this is two-fold. First, it is impossible to know exactly when the herring will arrive, although they are anticipated in mid-January. Second, most of the fishing takes place at night. The fishing boats arrive at sunset and haul in the last of their nets a few hours after sunrise. But if you are an early-morning riser and your timing is right, the sight is unique.

The Town

Even without the herring, Sausalito is an interesting town to visit. The rainy season is usually interspersed with a few days of false spring. These crisp, sunny days are perfect for wandering Sausalito's streets—looking in the many shop windows or hiking the pedestrian lanes that climb the steep hillsides.

Bay Model

In addition to browsing the shops and dining in one of the many interesting restaurants, you may want to visit a large-scale model of the entire San Francisco Bay and Delta waters. The Bay Model is operated by the U. S. Army Corps of Engineers to study the effects of tides and currents. It is located at the far end of Sausalito, near the 2100 block of Bridgeway. Admission is free.

For more information on the Bay Model consult the Ready Reference—Celebrations & Outings (Sausalito).

February

California Sea Lion

February Gardening

In Bloom

Annuals: calendula, Iceland poppy, pansy, and sweet William
Perennials: cineraria, cyclamen, primrose, and violet
Bulbs: hyacinth, narcissus, and tulip
Flowering trees: acacia and magnolia
Shrubs: azalea, camellia, and Scotch broom

Complete winter pruning of dormant plants, such as cane berries, fruit trees, grapes, roses, and wisteria. Do not delay; warming weather will soon send these plants into a vigorous growth spurt which you want to direct by pruning.

Complete winter dormant spraying of fruit trees and roses. When the leaves and blossoms begin to emerge from the swelling buds, it is too late for dormant spraying.

Continue to pick up fallen camellia flowers in order to prevent the spread of camellia petal blight.

Destroy snails and slugs. Warming weather will soon lure these slimy regiments into destructive garden maneuvers.

Garden Catalogs

A February pleasure is the leisurely browsing of garden catalogs. Most catalogs are an agreeable education and give bits of advice among the plant descriptions. Several catalogs, such as Burpee's and Park's, are more colorfully illustrated than most garden reference books. It is an easy way to familarize yourself with a variety of flowers, fruit trees, and vegetables.

Another advantage of catalog browsing is to become acquainted with plants seldom, if ever, encountered in local nurseries. For example, the Burpee catalog lists 24 varieties of strawberries, among them the small woodland alpine strawberries. These choice tart strawberries are considered a seasonal delicacy in Europe. Alpine (*fraises de bois*) strawberries thrive in the Bay Area. You can buy either plants (expensive) or seeds (cheap but difficult to germinate). Other catalogs also carry alpine strawberries.

A variety of catalogs are listed in the Ready Reference—Gardening under garden catalogs. Specialized catalogs are listed under herbs, iris, and wildflowers. Write for them soon. April and May, prime planting time, will soon be here.

In the Nursery Look for:

Annuals: forget-me-not, snapdragon, stock, and sweet William
Perennials: cineraria, candytuft, gazania, and primrose
Shrubs: azalea, camellia and rhododendron
Bare-root plants: cane berries, fruit trees, roses
Bulb-like: amaryllis, tuberous begonia, calla, gladiolus, and lily

Nurserymen will soon plant bare-root plants in containers and sell them later at a higher price, so buy and plant bare-root roses and fruit trees now. For cane berries see page 19.

February is also a good month for buying container-grown citrus trees. Remember citrus (particularly grapefruit and orange) need high summer heat to develop a sweet fruit. If your summers are influenced by cooling bay weather, plant your citrus in a sheltered area where sunlight is reflected off a white or light colored wall. The Meyer lemon thrives in the Bay Area where other citrus fail—the fruit of a Meyer lemon is mild and slightly sweet.

Plant summer bulbs and bulb-like plants such as, agapanthus, amaryllis, callas, cannas, gladiolus, and tuberous begonias.

The cheery, multi-colored English primrose (*Primula polyantha*) is in full bloom. This small perennial flower is easy to take care of and gives a second set of blooms if you cut it back one-third to one-half when it finishes blooming. Plant it in the sun or semi-shade. A primrose will multiply to give you more plants.

If you did not divide overgrown summer perennials such as Shasta daisies last fall, now is a good time to do it.

Azaleas, Camellias, and Rhododendron

Azaleas and camellias are in bloom and rhododendron are in the budding stage. Now, while they are dormant and you can see the bloom color, is an excellent time to purchase and plant these beautiful landscape shrubs which thrive in the Bay Area. All grow slowly, so look for pleasing form and leaves as well as blooms. All three are acid-loving plants which need rich soil (add plenty of peat moss or leaf mold) that drains quickly. Plant high, with the top of the root ball slightly above the soil. All three love a thick mulch (two inches), particularly of acid-producing pine needles or oak leaves. Plant with other water-loving plants to help confine water use to a limited area.

Strawberries

Strawberries are highly rewarding, attractive, and easy-to-care-for plants. Plop a few in pots, plant a patch, or border a flower bed with them; 25 plants will yield 20 to 30 quarts of strawberries, enough for a family of five.

Plant strawberries in sunny, well-drained, humus-rich soil. They are usually grown in rows on raised mounds 5 inches high and 30 inches from the center of one row to the center of the next row. Important: plant with the crown just above the soil level and the roots just below the soil level. Pine needles make a lovely beneficial mulch: strawberries like the acid and the needles keep the strawberries off the ground in addition to keeping the soil moist. Replace strawberries every three years from new plants formed on the runners. Either let the runner root in the strawberry patch or place a small pot of soil under the forming plant and snip off runner when rooted.

Recommended varieties for Bay Area gardens:

Sequoia is an outstanding strawberry for local growing. It is prolific, vigorous, beautiful, and favorful; plus it is resistant to many diseases.

Quinault is a large, tasty berry favored by Chez Panisse chefs for desserts. It produces an abundance of runners.

Tioga is an elongated strawberry good for preserves and freezing. It is somewhat resistant to virus but highly susceptible to verticillium wilt (see note under raspberries on facing page).

Cane Berries

Cane berries are available this month in bare-root form. All cane berries need plenty of water and in the Bay Area are best in full sun. To plant, dig a trench, add plenty of compost or humus plus wood ashes (potash), and mix well. Dig a hole for each plant (2 feet apart for raspberries, 4 feet apart for blackberries) and make a pointed cone of soil in each hole. Sit plant on top of cone and fan roots around cone; then cover with soil. Allow 4 feet between rows. Cane berries need a trellis or fence to support the long arching canes. Each winter cut off canes that have fruited, leaving young canes to produce next year's fruit.

Raspberries are expensive to buy but easy to grow. Several varieties recommended for the Bay Area are:
'**Heritage**' is everbearing*, with two main crops in July and September. It also has tasty fruit, and vigorous, stiff canes.
'**Indian Summer**' is everbearing* with two crops. It is also vigorous with large, soft, tasty fruit.

Blackberries are thornier and more invasive than raspberries. Several varieties recommended for the Bay Area are:
'**Boysen**' has a large, sweet-tart, aromatic berry of excellent flavor. It is also vigorous and bears an early crop.
'**Ollalie**' has a large, shiny, black, firm, and sweet berry. It is productive with thorny canes. It resists verticillium wilt and mildew.
'**Marion**' has a medium-size blackberry with long vigorous, very thorny canes. Plant it closer than other blackberries, 2-½ feet apart.
Warning: Any tiny piece of blackberry will sprout a new plant. Keep your blackberries under control or they will create a thorny, strangling patch.

*Everbearing berries produce a few berries throughout the season with several crops of many berries.

Verticillium Wilt

Note: Raspberries are susceptible to verticillium wilt, a soil-borne fungus disease that unfortunately thrives in the Bay Area. The invaded plant will wilt, turning yellow from the base upward. Some plants survive. There is no home remedy except to plant resistent varieties. The blackberry 'Ollalie' is resistant to verticillium wilt.

February Foods

Dandelion Greens

This is the one time of the year you need not curse the dandelion weeds (*Taraxacum officinale*). The young, tender dandelion leaves—formed before the yellow flowers appear—have a refreshing, bitter flavor. If you tie the leaves together in the garden, the interior leaves will blanch like endive. Dig up the plant, including the root, just before you want to eat it. Use only the tender interior leaves. Dandelion leaves are wonderful tossed in a salad or braised in bacon fat or butter for a few minutes.

Avocados

Avocados are abundant and inexpensive in February. The thin-skinned, medium green 'Fuerte' is a winter avocado with a distinctive pear shape. The rounder less flavorful 'Bacon' is also a winter avocado. Avoid avocados with cracks or dark bruised spots. A bruised avocado is not just unsightly, it also has an unpleasant bitter taste. An avocado will ripen more quickly when it is wrapped in a paper bag. It is ripe when it yields slightly when gently squeezed.

Monterey Prawn (Spot Shrimp)

Beautiful, pale-red prawns from Monterey are available at fish markets from spring into fall. Like all shellfish, prawns (as large shrimps are commonly called) are ruined by overcooking. These large shellfish are delicious grilled or sauteed.

Stir-Frying Winter Vegetables

A large Asian population in the Bay Area assures us a fresh and abundant supply of oriental winter vegetables seldom found elsewhere in the United States. The facing page discusses many of these vegetables. The Chinese cooking method called stir-frying quickly produces perfectly cooked vegetables. Stir-fried vegetables are often combined with small amounts of meat to make economical main dishes.

Non-oriental vegetables, particularly winter vegetables, such as cabbage, celery, broccoli, spinach, and Swiss chard, are excellent when stir-fried. While you can stir-fry in an ordinary skillet, a wok is better. Sturdy, inexpensive woks can be bought in Chinatown hardware stores. You should also buy a large, wide, flat Chinese spatula, which makes tossing the vegetables easy.

Stir-Frying Technique

① Cut all vegetables and meat in a uniform manner and size.

② Heat about 2 tablespoons of oil (peanut or corn oil is preferred) in the wok to the point of fragrance—just before it begins to smoke.

③ Add the vegetables and quickly toss to coat them in oil; this is called greening the vegetables and it seals in the flavor and juices. Remove the vegetables immediately and set aside.

④ Add the meat and toss it in the hot oil until almost done.

⑤ Add the vegetables to the meat and toss them until done. You can also add flavoring: soy sauce, oyster sauce, stock, salt, Szechwan pepper, sherry, shredded ginger, catsup, vinegar, or cornstarch dissolved in equal amounts of liquid.

Oriental Vegetables

Bean curd (tofu) is a custard-like square of pressed soybeans. Bland in flavor, it is excellent fried with vegetables, and flavored with soy sauce. It is high in protein.

Bok choy is a Chinese vegetable somewhat like celery. It is crunchy when stir-fried. It is also called Chinese cabbage—a misnomer since it is not part of the cabbage family.

Napa cabbage is a pale, elongated true Chinese cabbage. The Chinese take it out of the refrigerator the day before cooking—as it wilts it turns sweeter. Stir-fry or use uncooked in salads.

Ginger root is a pungent spice used grated or sliced thin. In February and March, and again in August, smooth, pink-skinned, young ginger is available. Store refrigerated in a thick, brown paper bag.

Icicle radish is a large, hefty radish often used shredded and cooked. It does not taste like the little finger-size icicle radish.

Lotus root is a potato-shaped rhizome which grows under water. Slice it thin to show off its lacy interior pattern either cooked or raw.

Mung bean sprouts should be fresh, plump, and unwilted. They combine well with a wide variety of other vegetables.

Mustard greens are a tangy, sharp-flavored vegetable usually stir-fried with pork.

Chinese parsley (cilantro, coriander) is an aromatic, strong-flavored herb. People either love or hate its flavor.

Snow peas are crisp, slightly sweet, wonderfully flavored peas eaten with the pod. Stir-fry them adding a little water to steam.

February Celebrations

Chinese New Year—San Francisco

Chinese New Year is probably the most important holiday for many Chinese. It is a combination of Christmas, Thanksgiving, and the Fourth of July with gifts, feasts, and fireworks. The date varies since the Chinese calendar is based on the lunar year, but the Chinese New Year is usually in February. The celebration continues for several days and ends with the Feast of Lanterns.

In Chinatown, branches from quince trees and peach trees are sold to bring good luck to the recipient. Red-flowered plants and orange-colored fruits are also sold—red and orange are good luck colors. Firecrackers are lit to scare away last year's evil.

The Chinese names for many of the foods served during this holiday are homonyms for auspicious words. For example, the Cantonese way of saying orange sounds like the word for wealth, and the word for tangerine sounds like the word for good luck. Kumquats are thought to bring wealth since kum sounds like the Chinese word for gold.

Traditionally, married adults give children and unmarried adults small red envelopes (*lai see bau*) containing money. The traditional greeting is *Gung hay fat choy* which translates to "Happiness and prosperity to you."

The big event is the grand noisy parade featuring colorful Chinese lions (mythical creatures that look more like Pekinese dogs than lions) and ending with the long snake-like dragon. Once only the royal family could display the dragon, which symbolized imperial power. Now the appearance of the dragon welcomes the new year. Crowds estimated at about 400,000 people squeeze into the narrow streets of San Francisco's Chinatown to watch the two-mile-long procession.

The festive Chinese New Year spirit can also be felt in the Chinatown areas of Oakland and Sacramento. Just as in San Francisco's Chinatown, special foods and plants are sold during the days preceding Chinese New Year. Expect parking to be difficult, restaurants to be crowded, and the streets to be popping with firecrackers tossed by giggling boys.

Chinese Spring Festival—San Francisco

In conjunction with Chinese New Year, the Chinese Cultural Center at 750 Kearny Street presents a celebration of Chinese folk arts. There are demonstrations of folk and classical music and dance, martial arts, and lion dancing.

Peach Blossom Festival, Dolls Festival—Los Altos Hills

Two Japanese celebrations are combined—the *Momono Sekku* (Peach Blossom Festival) and the *Hinamatsure* (Dolls Festival). In addition to a display of dolls and kimonos, there are demonstrations of Washi doll making, flower arranging, and brush painting. This is a small, one-day festival held at Foothill College, 12345 El Monte Road, Los Altos Hills.

February's blustery weather lends itself to three winter events—a dog sled competition, a snow carnival, and a clam chowder cookoff.

Dog Sled Races—Truckee

The Sierra Sweepstakes Dog Sled Races, held at the Truckee-Tahoe Airport, are the largest dog sled competition in California. The races are fun to watch, but all those barking dogs are noisy. It is best to leave your own dog at home.

Winterskol—Incline Village

Incline Village, a resort village at Lake Tahoe, hosts a winter carnival the first week of February. The event includes many snow activities and ends with a celebrity ski race.

Clam Chowder Cook-off—Santa Cruz

Within sight of the pounding surf, the annual Clam Chowder Cook-off is held every year at the Santa Cruz Boardwalk, located at Beach Street and Riverside Avenues. While in Santa Cruz, make an excursion to Natural Bridges State Beach to see the monarch butterflies hanging (or awakening) from their dense clusters in trees—see pages 160 and 161.

Remember the day, even the month, of an event may change. For more information consult the Ready Reference—Celebrations & Outings (under individual headings).

February Outings

Elephant Seals

The Seals of Año Nuevo

Fifty-five miles south of San Francisco is the Año Nuevo State Reserve—located on Highway 1 near the Gazos Creek Road just north of Santa Cruz.

The star of Año Nuevo is definitely the elephant seal—a natural wonder, an improbable animal. To protect the elephant seals as well as the public, viewers are led on tours by volunteer guides. The seals are such a popular attraction that it is necessary to make a reservation for the tours through Ticketron. Without a reservation there may not be space for you on the tours or you may have to wait hours. Dress warmly, wear comfortable walking shoes, and take binoculars.

The Elephant Seal

The largest of the earless seals, a male (bull) elephant seal can reach 22 feet in length and weigh up to 5,000 pounds.

Compare a male elephant seal with a California sea lion, the star performer of zoos and circuses—who also basks on the beaches of Año Nuevo Island. The male California sea lion measures up to 8 feet long and weighs up to 600 pounds. The California sea lion is illustrated on the cover page of the February section. To get an idea of how big an elephant seal is when viewed in person, imagine a garden slug the size of a hippopotamus and you begin to approach its remarkable size.

The Snout That Bellows

The male elephant seal's most notable feature is a snout of cavernous tissue, a flabby pendant, which normally hangs flaccid but can be inflated with air like a tubular balloon. Another notable feature of the elephant seal is his bellow. He tightly inflates his snout, and when he releases the air, it produces a deep and melancholy roar. It is the sort of sound that would make the hair on your neck rise were not this elephant seal basking on the beach so obviously docile.

Disposition

If you disturb an elphant seal's much loved sleep, odds are he will merely swish his fore flippers to send a shower of pebbles and sand at you with remarkable accuracy. Having accomplished this maneuver, he will simply fall asleep again. They can, however, move faster than you can run.

Elephant seals are sociable. They are gregarious by nature, roving in herds with the change of the season. In fact they are here for the winter season for mating.

Battles

Many of the bulls fight prodigious battles for the harem. If you scrutinize the male elephant seals, you will see the vivid, often blood-red battle scars from the current mating season's fighting and old scars from past compaigns.

The defeated males end up on Loser's Beach. The victorious males and their harems are out on the point where the main nursery at Año Nuevo is located.

February Outings

Harbor Seals

Other Seals of Año Nuevo

From the point of Año Nuevo, if the fog does not intervene, a pair of binoculars helps bring additional elephant seal victors and their harems into view over on the island. While you are looking at the island you will probably see other seals too.

You may see the agile dark-brown seal—which is not a true seal but the California sea lion. Unlike true seals, they can rotate their hind flippers from front to back, which makes them star circus performers. They are also identified by their external ears and big eyes.

You may also see the harbor seal (smaller than the sea lion, about 100 pounds.) They have spots and are sometimes called the common seal. The harbor seals are some of the smallest coastal seals, and they prefer calm, protected harbor water. During the late summer months, another seal, the tawny Stellar sea lion, mates at Año Nuevo.

Año Nuevo Reserve

Año Nuevo is one of the most interesting areas along the Northern California coastline. Once known for its treacherous hidden reefs and turbulent waters (many a ship went down here), it is now known for its seals. The nearly 1,252-acre reserve includes both beach and woodland—a game refuge for over 300 species of birds as well as the seals.

The Tour

The walk from the parking lot at Año Nuevo State Reserve to the point is 1 mile. The tour itself is approximately 3 miles. On the way out to the dunes, you may see the graceful black cormorant or an occasional pelican. See November Outings—Sonoma Coast for more information on Northern California sea birds.

Coastal Indians

Once you reach the dunes you will be treading on a bit of California history. These deep sand dunes cover Indian shell mounds where California Indians once discarded the hard seashells from the plentiful sea morsels upon which they dined. The abundant sea life, particularly abalone and rock fish, attracts the seals (seals are meat eaters) just as it did the Indians. Few visible signs remain of the coastal Indians who lived along the shoreline for thousands of years.

Año Nuevo Island

Once you reach the point, if the fog is not in, you can look across to Año Nuevo Island—located one-half mile off shore. The island is a game refuge and it is off-limits to visitors. It is also dangerous to try to visit the island. At minus tides, the surf is truly treacherous and several people have died trying to reach the island.

Timing Your Visit

The elephant seals are at Año Nuevo from approximately December through March. A series of visits permits you to see the fierce battles of the bulls, the mating, and the birth of the baby seals. Yearlings and molting adult seals remain in the spring and the summer.

For more information, consult the Ready Reference—Celebrations & Outings (Año Nuevo).

February Outings

In Search of Snow

When the weather is cold enough and the conditions are right, snow falls on the highest summits in the Bay Area. Mount Diablo (main peak 3,849 feet), Mount Tamalpais (2,650 feet at the highest peak), and Mount Hamilton (4,209 feet at the summit) are all candidates for snow.

Snow Areas

Most likely, however, a search for snow will lead us out of the Bay Area. Most of the snow resort areas are located around Lake Tahoe in the high Sierra. To the south of Lake Tahoe are Dodge Ridge and Badger Pass. Mount Lassen and Mount Shasta are to the north.

Whatever the direction, carry snow chains and have advance reservations. Bring sunglasses and suntan lotion—the high elevation and the reflective quality of snow make the sun's intensity up to four times as great as on a bright day at sea level.

Skiing

Alpine skiing, also called downhill skiing, is the form of skiing best known to Californians. But Nordic, or cross-country, skiing is becoming more popular because it is cheaper and the trails are less crowded.

Nordic Skiing

Nordic ski trails are mapped out with scenic beauty in mind—through forests, around lakes, and to places with spectacular views. Cross-country skiing by moonlight is an incredible experience—the countryside takes on a beautiful and eerie black and white quality.

Some Nordic ski resorts use a machine to tamp down the snow into narrow tracks so the skier can glide over the trail easily. There are also marked-but-ungroomed trails (many resorts offer a map) and some resorts patrol their trails. Tours are often available.

Resorts

For both Alpine and Nordic skiing, write or telephone the snow areas that interest you. The tourist bureaus listed under snow in the Ready Reference can direct you to individual resorts. Many resorts offer package plans that include accommodations, ski fees, and sometimes meals. Mid-week specials are common. Ski lessons are available at most resorts, either individual or group.

Snowshoeing

Snowshoeing is a relatively inexpensive although strenuous winter sport. There are several types of snowshoes ranging from short and round to the long and narrow with turned-up toes. In addition to snowshoes and bindings, an ice ax or ski poles are needed.

Several national parks provide free snowshoe walks. Lassen Volcanic Park Ski Area provides free use of snowshoes on walks to the Sulphur Works thermal area. At Badger Pass, snowshoes may be rented for walks led by rangers. Calaveras Big Trees State Park also has walks led by rangers, but you must provide your own snowshoes.

Winter in the Great Parks

There are a variety of national and state parks within a day's drive from the Bay Area that offer winter activities. Phone before driving to determine the weather and road conditions.

Lassen Volcanic Park Ski Area to the north of the Bay Area (about a 5 ½-hour drive) offers both Nordic skiing and snowshoe tours. The tours are led by a ranger-naturalist, including tours into the steaming mist of the Sulfur Works thermal area.

Yosemite, about 200 miles east of the Bay Area (about a 5-hour drive in the winter), becomes a winter fantasy-land under an icing of snow. It is both stunning and peaceful. The outdoor ice-rink at Curry Village has a fire in a pit at night.

On weekends, there are Nordic ski and snowshoe tours of the Tuolumne Grove of giant sequoias. There are also snowshoe tours of the Mariposa Grove. Nearby Badger Pass, the state's oldest ski area, offers Alpine skiing. There are even snow-cat rides.

Sequoia and **Kings Canyon National Parks**, about 250 miles southeast of the Bay Area (about a 7-hour drive) are spectacular in winter when the giant sequoia groves are snow bound and uncrowded. Nordic skiing is available at both parks and there are ranger-led snowshoe tours, as well as several snow play areas.

Calaveras Big Trees State Park, about 125 miles east of the Bay Area (about a 3-hour drive), offers both Nordic ski and showshoe tours led by rangers through the giant sequoias.

For more information consult the Ready Reference—Celebrations & Outings (snow and individual headings).

February Outings

San Francisco's Japan Center

When February weather is blustery, Japantown is convenient because you can park underneath the Japan Center complex (enter either on Geary or Post) and take an elevator up to weather-proof dining and shopping.

The Japan Center consists of several levels of inter-connected buildings. Begin your tour in the East Building with the huge, colorful Ginza Imports. Their display of oriental china and porcelain (both Chinese and Japanese) is vast and varied. Ginza Imports and the surrounding shops also feature oriental clothing and handicrafts.

Next, cross the covered Peace Plaza where performers entertain for free many Saturday afternoons—view the five-tier, 100-foot high Peace Pagoda before entering the Kintetsu Building and Restaurant Mall. Here a variety of Japanese restaurants border a twisting cobblestone lane. Just as in Japan, many restaurants display either photographs or plastic models of the foods they serve.

Then cross the covered, shop-lined Webster Street Bridge, noticing the Japanese dollmaking school and art galleries before entering the West Building. One of the most interesting shops is Kinokuniya, a large Japanese bookstore that sells beautiful calendars; also peek into the two pastry shops, one Japanese and the other European.

Japanese-style Soak

The Kabuki Hot Spring at 1750 Geary Boulevard is part of the Japanese Center. It is an invigorating experience. For a modest sum, on the sakura plan, you wash off Japanese style, toast yourself in the sauna (180 °F), then plunge into the chilling mizuburo tub (55 to 60 °F), and finally dip into the communal furo (100 to 110 °F). For more money, you can enjoy a vigorous shiatsu massage and a private room. The communal bath alternates days between men and women.

Buchanan Mall

From the Pagoda across Post Street is Buchanan Mall with more shops. On the corner as you enter the mall is Soko Hardware (1698 Post) which sells fine bonsai-pruning and flower-arranging tools. Downstairs there is a large selection of kitchenware.

For addresses and telephone numbers, consult the Ready Reference—Celebrations & Outings (Japan Center).

Season of Wind and Fog

Temperature—cool
mid forties to high sixties

The great winds of the Bay Area are called westerlies. They blow in from the Pacific Ocean and heap sand into dunes and batter cypress into photogenic contortions. During March, April, and May the westerlies are at their mightiest, increasing the wind chill factor and making the cool temperatures seem colder as our body heat is literally blown away. Fortunately the westerlies' fierce assault alternates with calm days when moisture evaporates off the rain-soaked hills enfolding the Bay Area in a balmy haze.

Billowing Fog

This is the finest season for watching the fog drift in through the gaps in the coastal mountain range. The biggest gap is the Golden Gate. To the north, Estero Gap and the Gap at Elk Valley are the doors through which fog enters Marin County. To the south, San Bruno Gap and the Crystal Springs Gap are the portals for fog entering the San Francisco peninsula.

During this season a great fog bank forms off the coast. Water clings to minute salt particles tossed up by sea breezes which thicken into a vapor. Then, with the dwindling heat intensity of the late afternoon sun, it forms a ground-hugging cloud called fog which drifts in through the mountain gaps in beautiful, billowing shapes.

Sunny Days

However, the high sun-shielding fog of summer has yet to form and in May the morning and early afternoon sky is often clear and sunny, offering some of the most pleasant weather of the year.

Varied Excursions

Cold March days are perfect for escaping to the warm mud baths of Calistoga while warmer May days encourage longer excursions to Mendocino, or to Yosemite when the falls are still full from melting snow. It is also a time to watch spring's newborn pups paddle about their mothers in the kelp beds of Monterey—or to visit Audubon Canyon Ranch to see fledgling herons and egrets totter from their nests of sticks.

31

Seasonal Reminders

In addition to the outings recommended for March, April and May, the following phenomena provide alternative seasonal excursions.

Elephant Seals

Many elephant seals remain at Año Nuevo through March. See February outings pages 24 to 27.

Pacific Gray Whales

Pacific gray whales migrate north along the Pacific coast through April. See January outings pages 10 to 11. March is a good month to observe the migration.

March

Sea Otter

March Gardening

In Bloom

Annuals: calendula, sweet alyssum, and pansy
Perennials: cineraria, candytuft, gazania, primrose, and violet
Trees: acacia, fruit, hawthorn, and tulip
Shrubs: azalea, camellia, ceanothus, and Scotch broom
Bulbs: hyacinth, narcissus, and tulip

Bluegrass, fescue, and rye lawns have their most active growth spurt this month. Fertilize them with lawn food, and reseed bald patches. Prepare ground for a new lawn but wait until the heavy rains are finished to seed it.

Weeding is easy now because the soil is damp and the weeds young.

Destroy snails and slugs by giving them to the birds at your local duck pond.

Rolled up newspapers left overnight in the garden collect earwigs which can then be gathered and put in the garbage can.

This is a good month to apply all-purpose fertilizer to all plants except for ones that require a special fertilizer. For example, fertilize citrus with a citrus high-nitrogen fertilizer that includes iron; iron chlorosis (yellowing) is a common problem in the Bay Area.

Fertilize roses and cover the ground around roses with a mulch leaving a mulch-free space around the rose stem.

Fuchsias

At the end of this month, when the danger of frost is past, prune fuchsias by removing last summer's growth, but leave two swelling leaf buds on each pruned branch. Severe pruning helps control fuchsia mites. (Later when active growth starts, pinch off the tips to make the plant fuller.) Fertilize them.

Azaleas, Camellias, and Rhododendrons

After blooming prune leggy camellias at the point where each branch swells; this encourages a fuller, more attractive growth pattern. Tidy up azalea plants after they bloom by pruning back stray or uneven growth. Pick off all withered rhododendron flowers; take care not to injure growth just below the flower. Fertilize camellias, azaleas, and rhododendrons with an acid fertilizer. Mulch with pine needles or oak leaves, if they are available.

In the Nursery Look for:

Annuals: ageratum, impatiens, lobelia, marigold, snap dragon and stock
Perennials: cineraria, gazania, pelargonium, and primrose.
Bulb-like: amaryllis, tuberous begonia, calla, canna, dahlia, gladiolus, tigridia,
*   and watsonia*
Flowering trees
Shrubs: azalea and camellia

Set out landscaping plants such as ground covers, shrubs, and trees so that the warming spring weather hastens their growth.

Plant summer bulbs, corms, and tubers such as, agapanthus, amaryllis, tuberous begonia, calla, canna, dahlia, gladiolus, tigridia, and watsonia.

Plant flowering annuals and perennials. Spring blooming: cinerarias, poppies, primroses, and violets. Summer blooming: ageratums, lobelias, marigolds, pansies, petunias, snapdragons, and stocks. Wait to plant heat-thriving plants such as asters and zinnias.

Ceanothus

Ceanothus, also known as California lilacs, are a valuable addition to most gardens because of their easy-to-care-for natures and their glorious flowers. Ceanothus generally bloom in March and April (some bloom earlier or later) so now is a good time to select them at the nursery. Flower colors range from intense violet-blue to delicate pale blues to whites and an occasional rose or pale pink. A large ceanothus in full bloom is spectacular; as eye-catching as a flowering plum, it seems to be an explosion of color.

Because ceanothus are native to California, they are adapted to rain-less summers. In fact, after their first year of establishing themselves in the garden, most ceanothus need to be watered only every other month during the dry season. Too much water in summer shortens their life span, so don't plant them where sprinklers will reach them.

There are many ceanothus species and cultivars, ranging from low spreading ground covers to sprawling shrubs to small trees. They prefer sloping sites where drainage is good, and they generally like full sun.

For gardens visited by deer, select a ceanothus with small leaves which are less attractive to deer.

March Foods

Sorrel

Sorrel is a relatively unknown green vegetable (actually a grass). Sometimes called sourgrass, it has a distinctively sour, almost lemony taste. It
cooks quickly and makes a splendid soup. It is best to cook it with other
greens such as chard, mustard green, or spinach since sorrel turns rather
brown when cooked. A few sorrel leaves add a tangy bite to a mixed
green salad. It is available in many produce markets. A wild variety of
sorrel grows as a weed in many Bay Area gardens.

Radicchio

Radicchio is a Northern Italian salad green with a pretty crimson-colored
leaf and a form that resembles a small, loose-leaf cabbage. It has a slightly
bitter, nutty taste similar to Belgian endive (to which it is related botani-
cally). It is used with other salad greens to add variety of color and flavor.
It can also be braised or barbecued.

Radicchio is not truly seasonal, although it is harvested more frequently in winter and spring. It is discussed here because it is a food new
to most Northern Californian cooks and it is becoming a popular item in
California cuisine. It is sold by gourmet produce markets—at a premium
price. The radicchio flown in from Italy tends to have a brighter red
color than the radicchio grown in California. It can be easily grown from
seed in Bay Area gardens.

Asparagus

Asparagus grows in the rich peat soil of the Sacramento River Delta.
Local greengrocers carry Delta asparagus through May. Look for tightly
closed tops, a bright green color, and a white end which is not more than
one-third of the asparagus in length. Hand-select asparagus with the
same circumference so they will cook in the same amount of time. Fat
spears or skinny spears does not matter—both have their fans.

Recipes for cooking asparagus found in many cookbooks would aston-
ish most Bay Area cooks. The asparagus available to us is so fresh, young,
and tender that we do not have to peel off the green skin which is tough
and bitter on older asparagus. Cut or snap off the white ends of each
stalk. Bay Area cooks usually steam asparagus without tying them in
bunches, or else they saute them in butter with a little water. Do not
overcook asparagus. Perfectly cooked asparagus is bright green and
crisp, not yellow-green and mushy.

Bay Area Shellfish

Cool, brisk March days are suited to hot soups with shellfish such as San Francisco's cioppino, or the French *bouillabaisse*. The necessary crabs, clams, mussels, and rockfish are all available fresh. The season for various Bay Area shellfish varies greatly—the following is a general orientation.

Dungeness crabs are available fresh from October to June. Crabs are usually bought already cooked and cracked. Always buy the largest crab available, about three pounds, for the finest flavor.

Delta crayfish are fresh water cousins to lobsters. They can be bought alive in the Delta area (see the Ready Reference—Foods, Delta crayfish) from May through October.

Shrimp. Large shrimp, commonly called prawns, come from Monterey Bay. Tiny bay shrimp are plentiful—sold already cooked—they are great in salads, in a curry, or stuffed in an avocado or an artichoke.

Abalone are pried off rocks by skin divers. They are carefully regulated in California and difficult to obtain. Pound them prior to cooking, then saute them quickly over high heat. Aquaculture may bring back this delicious shellfish to the marketplace.

Clams. Markets usually sell eastern littleneck and cherrystone clams. You can dig your own local clams at several California beaches.* Look for posted signs warning of "red tide" which can be lethally poisonous. Pismo clams are wonderfully sweet and tender—before eating them remove their stomachs. The delectable razor clams should have the dark parts removed. Discard all clams that float, or have broken shells, or refuse to shut their shells tightly.

Mussels. Markets usually sell eastern mussels. From November through April you can pry off your own local mussels from beach rocks at low tide*. To be safe look for quarantine signs. Discard any mussel that remains open after a 2-minute vacation in the freezer.

Oysters. Most markets sell bluepoint oysters from the East and Gulf coasts. Our own native Olympia oyster has been overrun by the cultivated Pacific oyster which is grown in Tomales Bay. (See August Foods and the Ready Reference—Foods under oysters.)

Squid. A fine tasting squid comes from Monterey Bay. Squids make an inexpensive and tasty meal once you learn how to clean them. They are available fresh from April through October.

* Fishing license required for those over 16.

March Celebrations

San Francisco Orchid Society Show—San Francisco

In March many cymbidiums bloom, and it's time for the largest West Coast orchid show, held every year in San Francisco. In fact, the show grew so large that in 1989 it moved from the San Francisco County Fair Building to Fort Mason. Several thousand orchid plants are exhibited and sold; there are also educational displays on orchid growing. This is an opportunity to purchase orchids that are difficult to obtain. Also look in the gardening index under orchids for several Bay Area orchid growers who sell rare orchids and conduct classes.

Macy's Spring Flower Show—San Francisco

The downtown Macy's store at Stockton and O'Farrell streets is adorned with locally grown and exotic flower displays. These displays are based on a different theme each year. The wonderful rhododendrons and azaleas that form the basis for many of the displays are grown and maintained year after year for Macy's—they are quite spectacular. The show takes place about a week before Easter, so the date varies. Sometimes the show lasts for two weeks.

Ikebana Flower Shows—San Francisco, Oakland

The Japanese art of flower arranging (*Ikebana*) uses symbolism to express a deep experience of life. Shows are held at Oakland's Lakeside Park and at San Francisco's County Fair Building.

Vernal Equinox—approximately March 21

The Vernal (spring) Equinox is one of two days each year when the sun crosses the plane of the earth's equator, making day and night the same length all over the world. The Vernal Equinox also marks the beginning of spring.

St. Patrick's Day—March 17

This is the feast day of St. Patrick, who was a Christian missionary to Ireland in the fifth century. A national holiday in Ireland, St. Patrick's Day is celebrated by Irishmen all over the world. It is traditional to wear something green. There is an annual snake race at Zellerbach Plaza (located at Bush and Market) in San Francisco at noon on March 17. In San Francisco, a St. Patrick's Day Parade begins about noon on the Sunday nearest March 17—the parade has Irish pipers and many marching bands. There are also parades in Oakland and Sacramento.

Camellia Festival—Sacramento

As the Camellia Capital of the World, Sacramento's camellia festival includes: camellia flower exhibits, a parade, a grand ball, and a folk dancing pageant. Capitol Park in Sacramento has more than 800 varieties of camellias in bloom during February and March.

Cherry Trees—San Francisco

From approximately the last week of March into the first week of April, the cherry trees are in bloom in the Japanese Tea Garden in San Francisco's Golden Gate Park.

Daffodil Hill—Volcano

In the gold country near Volcano, more than 200 species of daffodils bloom during late March and early April (April Outings page 61).

Spring Blossom Festival—Healdsburg

The Spring Blossom Festival provides a self-guided tour through Alexander Valley (near Healdsburg) as fruit trees and flowers blossom. It has exhibits, country luncheons, and entertainment.

Nikkei Matsuri—San Jose

The Japanese American Spring Festival in San Jose has cultural exhibits, demonstrations, arts, crafts, food, and entertainment.

Snowfest—North Lake Tahoe

The North Lake Tahoe-Truckee Snowfest lasts nine days. It begins the first Saturday of March. This celebration of the winter season includes more than 60 events such as a torch light parade down the slopes of Squaw Valley, fireworks over Tahoe City, street dancing, arm wrestling, ski races, and a pancake breakfast.

Junior Grand National—San Francisco

Timed to coincide with Easter vacation, the Junior Grand National is three shows in one—a livestock exhibit, a high school rodeo, and a horse show (both English and Western classes.)

Remember the day, even the month, of an event may change from year to year. For more information consult the Ready Reference—Celebrations & Outings.

March Outings

Calistoga

If blustery March weather is depressing, consider a rejuvenating trip through Napa Valley to the steaming hot geysers, mineral springs, and mud baths of Calistoga. Over the years Napa Valley has taken on an elegant, almost European charm. But not Calistoga. Calistoga is pure Americana. Bordering on a western or a frontier appearance, it is a small town that reminds many people of "the good old days."

The Mud Baths

The spas offer similar treatments with mud and mineral waters. First you submerge yourself, reclining in an individual mud bath of mineral water mixed with white volcanic ash powder heated to a little over 100 °F. The hot mud is quite relaxing and is said to draw out toxins from the skin. After wallowing in the mud, you shower, then soak in heated mineral water with whirlpool or Jacuzzi jets. Then you proceed to a steam bath and a blanket wrap said to sweat out any remaining toxins.

For an additional fee you can end with a massage (30 minutes to 1½ hours). Several places offer different types of massages.

Swedish massage. Swedish massage is the most frequently encountered form of massage. It is a therapeutic body massage designed to relax the muscles.

Foot reflexology. Foot reflexology is a stimulation of various nerve points on the foot believed to correspond with organs and glands.

Acupressure massage. Acupressure massage is derived from acupuncture theory. Finger pressure is applied to various points on the body during the massage to help the body heal itself.

The spas generally resemble motels—most spas *are* also motels. The facilities are separate for men and women. All the spas are popular and frequently completely reserved weeks in advance.

Old Faithful Geyser

There are only a few regularly erupting geysers, and one—called Old Faithful—is just outside Calistoga. Every 40 minutes boiling water erupts, shooting 60 feet into the air. Admission is charged.

Soaring

Calistoga's Soaring Center, located right in town, possesses nearly ideal conditions for soaring in a motorless glider plane. The cost is moderate. Reservations are usually necessary on weekends.

Ballooning

An expensive but unforgettable experience is provided by a balloon ride up into the air to drift along surveying the valley below you in what has been called America's safest form of air transport. There are several balloon businesses near Calistoga.

Petrified Forest

Just outside Calistoga is the road to the Petrified Forest (admission charged). It is a forest of redwoods converted into stone that are estimated to be six million years old.

Robert Louis Stevenson

The Silverado Museum in St. Helena is dedicated to the life and work of former resident Robert Louis Stevenson. The Robert Louis Stevenson Park (which is basically undeveloped) is the honeymoon site of Stevenson and his bride Fanny. For a glimpse of life during Stevenson's time, visit the Sharpsteen Museum and the Sam Brannan Cottage in Calistoga. The museum features a three-dimensional diorama of Calistoga in 1856. The cottage is refurbished to look as it did during Stevenson's visit.

Jack London

To visit the Jack London State Historic Park turn onto Oakville Grade which leads to Dry Creek Road (veer right) and onto Trinity Road which ends on Route 12 near Glen Ellen and the park. The large stone house built by Charmain, London's wife, serves as a museum with mementos, papers, and furnishings belonging to the Londons. At the end of a three-quarter-mile trail are the ruins of Wolf House. Jack London built this dream house which burned to the ground before he occupied it. Admission is charged.

For more information on a visit to the Calistoga area consult the Ready Reference—Celebrations & Outings (Calistoga).

March Outings

Monterey

March is a good month to visit Monterey because of the newborn sea otters. But Monterey is interesting even without the sea otter pups. Monterey, first Spanish, then Mexican, and finally the first capital of California, is also the city that launched an architectural style of whitewashed, two-story adobes with balconies. The Monterey style incorporates features of both Spanish colonial and New England styles. The following is a brief guide to points of interest in Monterey.

Monterey State Historic Park

Recapture early California history with a visit to the Custom House where the 28-star U.S. flag was raised in 1846. Visit the Casa Del Oro (once saloon and general store) and Larkin House (Larkin was U.S. Consul in California from 1844 to 1846). Also see the French Boarding House where Robert Louis Stevenson lived and wrote in 1879, or the First Theater (1846) which still produces theatrical performances.

Monterey Bay Aquarium

One of the largest and most beautiful aquariums in the world is located at 886 Cannery Row. The magnificent kelp forest is mesmerizing, and so are the touch pools, aviary, octopus gallery, and sea otter exhibit.

Cannery Row

In the early 1940s million-dollar sardine catches supported 16 canneries along Cannery Row. In 1945, John Steinbeck's novel, *Cannery Row*, was published and from then on the world knew the old salts of "the row." But by 1947, the sardines disappeared and most of the canneries closed. Today you can pass beneath the old covered conveyor belts that once dispatched cans to the warehouse. The old buildings are now restaurants, shops, and galleries.

The Municipal Wharfs and Fishermen's Wharf

The Municipal Wharfs are working piers where fishing boats unload their catch. Four blocks away is Fishermen's Wharf with shops, restaurants, and excursion boats.

For more information on a trip to Monterey consult the Ready Reference— Celebrations & Outings (Monterey).

California Sea Otter

Once hundreds of thousands of sea otters (illustrated on the March cover page) inhabited areas from Baja California up the western coast of North America, across the Aleutian Islands, and down to Japan. In the eighteenth and nineteenth centuries, fur traders slaughtered the sea otter until it was considered to be extinct. Now there are fewer than 2,000 sea otters along the coast of California. However, there are many more sea otters in Alaska.

The sea otter is about 4 feet long and weighs about 55 pounds. Its hind feet are webbed and its front paws are dexterous like hands. Without an insulating layer of blubber the sea otter fluffs air into its thick luxurious fur in order to retain body heat. It dines on sea urchins, abalone, clams, crabs, and about 40 other sea tidbits. One of the few animal tool users, the sea otter uses a rock balanced on its chest to break open its catch of shell fish and sometimes holds a rock to use as a weight when diving. It consumes about 25 percent of its body weight in food each day.

March is an excellent month to view sea otters because the winter storms are past and the pups born between January and March are still small and adorable. One of the most enjoyable aspects of watching is to observe the devoted care a sea otter mother gives her pup. A mature female gives birth to one pup every other year. She spends much time grooming, feeding, and teaching her young. The mothers ferry their young around on their stomachs while floating on their backs.

Where to View the Sea Otter

Monterey:	Fisherman's Wharf	Carmel Point
	Municipal Wharf #2	
	Cannery Row	Pebble Beach: (17 Mile Drive)
	Coast Guard Breakwater	Point Joe
		Bird Rock
Pacific Grove:	Lover's Point	Cypress Point
	Otter Point	Pescadero Point
	Point Pinos	

Contact the Friends of the Sea Otter to obtain more information about sea otters. Their address is in the Ready Reference—Celebrations & Outings (California sea otter).

March Outings

Saratoga

Saratoga is a small, pleasant town tucked in the foothills of the Santa Cruz Mountains just west of San Jose. An outing to Saratoga is not a major expedition—it consists of visiting one of the several stylish boutiques, lunching at a European-style restaurant, and touring one or more of the special places discussed below that make an excursion to Saratoga worthwhile.

Saratoga is reached by taking Freeway 17 past San Jose to Highway 9, which is also known as the Saratoga and Los Gatos Road.

Hakone Japanese Gardens

Why visit Saratoga in March? Because the Hakone Japanese Gardens should be in bloom. The Hakone Japanese Gardens is located outside the town of Saratoga on Big Basin Way.

Hakone Japanese Gardens is considered to be the only authentic Japanese garden in the United States. The attention to detail at the Hakone gardens makes it a true Japanese garden art form.

A brochure available at Hakone Japanese Gardens describes it as "a hill and water garden in the strolling pond style typical of the Zen garden of the middle seventeenth century." Its attractions include a tea house, a pond, a waterfall, an arched bridge, a water pavilion, a sand and stone garden, and a moon viewing house.

Villa Montalvo Center For The Arts

The Villa Montalvo Center was formerly the estate of United States Senator and San Francisco Mayor James D. Phelan. The large Mediterranean villa now is a center for the arts, and a 175-acre public park.

Paul Masson Vineyards

In Saratoga the Paul Masson Champagne Cellars, located on Saratoga Avenue, offer daily tours and a wine tasting at the end of the tour.

The Mountain Winery of Paul Masson, located in the hills off Pierce Road, is the setting for a fine summer music concert series. The Romanesque entrance is believed to date from the sixteenth century; it was transported around Cape Horn from Spain.

For more information on a visit to Saratoga consult the Ready Reference— Celebrations & Outings (Saratoga).

April

Pacific Coast Iris

April Gardening

In Bloom

Annuals: California poppy, sweet alyssum, and pansy
Perennials: cineraria, candytuft, gazania, primrose, and violet
Trees: acacia, various fruit, hawthorn, and tulip
Shrubs: azalea, camellia, rhododendron, and rose
Rhizomes: calla and bearded iris
Wildflowers

Fruit trees develop fruit now. Thin the fruit when it is as big as a dime in order to produce larger fruit. Thinning also reduces the weight and consequent stress on young branches.

Continue to pull weeds while the ground is still soft from winter rains—later it will be more difficult.

Spray roses vigorously with water to destroy aphids.

Do not cut off the green foliage of bulbs that have just bloomed. The foliage produces the nutrients needed for next year's blooms. Remove foliage only when it turns brown. Hide fading foliage by covering it with spreading annuals such as petunia or verbena.

Tip-pinch fuchsia branches.

Take cuttings for new plants from azaleas, carnations, chrysanthemums, fuchsias, and geraniums. Root the cuttings in damp sand or vermiculite. Use healthy non-blooming stems for the cuttings. It helps to dip the cut end of the stem in a rooting hormone (available from a nursery).

Lawns

April is the month to fertilize lawns. Since the heavy rains are over, it is also a fine month to plant a new lawn from seed or sod. Both methods need careful preparation.

The Bay Area's varied climates are right on the borderline between cool season and subtropical grasses. Most areas can grow cool season grasses but with difficulty. Cool season grasses include: bent, blue (the classic green lawn), fescue, rye, redtop, and clover. In mild winter areas the cool season grasses are brownish in summer. They can be grown from seed or sod.

Subtropical grasses include: zoysia, St. Augustine, and bermuda. These lawns are usually grown from sprigs or stolons. Subtropical grasses turn brown in winter.

In the Nursery Look for:

Annuals: aster, impatiens, lobelia, marigold, petunia, and zinnia
Perennials: carnation, felicia, pelargonium, marguerite, and Shasta daisy
Bulb-like: tuberous begonia, calla, dahlia, gladiolus, and tigridia
Container-grown trees and shrubs
Herbs

The gardening season is beginning and nurseries are well-stocked. Since the danger of freezes is past, set out frost-vulnerable plants, such as bougainvillea and hibiscus, as well as other sunshine-lovers such as asters, dahlias, and zinnias.

If you did not prepare your vegetable and flower beds in March, do it now and refer to the deep-bed gardening techniques on page 35.

Summer Bulbs

Plant summer bulbs, corms, rhizomes, and tubers such as, agapanthus, amaryllis, tuberous begonias, callas, cannas, dahlias, gladiolus, and tigridia.

Summer Vegetable Garden

April and May are the best months in the Bay Area to plant your summer vegetable garden. Set out seedlings—particularly tomato plant seedlings—or sow seeds for beans, carrots, Swiss chard, corn, cucumbers and radishes. Refer to the May gardening section (pages 66 and 67) for a discussion of dependable Bay Area vegetables.

The Herb Garden

April is an excellent month to plant an herb garden. The following pages describe herbs easily grown in the Bay Area. Nurseries sell 4-inch pots of basic herbs such as anise, basil, caraway, chives, coriander, dill, lavender, marjoram, mint, oregano, parsley, rosemary, saffron, sage, savory, sesame, tarragon, and thyme.

From garden catalogs that specialize in herbs you can order the more exotic herbs and vegetables such as angelica, apple mint, fenugreek, sorrel, and yarrow. You can also add bitter arugula greens, rare flageolet beans (for cassoulet), racambole (Spanish shallot), and Egyptian onions. Catalogs that specialize in herbs are listed in the Ready Reference—Gardening (herbs).

April Gardening Extra

The Herb Garden

In the Bay Area the herbs listed below can be grown in a sunny spot in average soil. Do not worry about an ideal climate. Every herb, except French tarragon, can be grown from seed. But it is much easier to start with a 4-inch potted plant from a nursery.

Basil—(annual)

Sweet basil, a leafy, compact 12-inch high annual, is easy to grow. Keep pinching back the tips to make it bushy. The pungent, peppery taste is the basis for the Italian pesto sauce. 'Dark Opal' is an attractive, mild flavored, and purple-tinged variety. Water basil well and watch out for snails.

Bay—(evergreen)

A bay tree grows so slowly it thrives in a large pot for years. The fragrant leaves are used for flavoring soups, sauces, marinades, and in a bouquet garni. The Turkish plant (Laurus nobilis) has a milder flavor than the California bay (Umbellularia californica).

Chives—(perennial)

A handsome green porcupine of a plant(12 to 15 inches high), chives are also very easy to grow. Clip off some of the mild onion-flavored leaves and add them to eggs, baked potatoes, dips, salads, and soups.

Dill—(annual)

Dill is a large (4 feet high) plant with lacy leaves. The leaves have a mild flavor and are beautiful sprinkled over potato salad or fish. The seeds have a sharp, bitter taste, and are used in pickle brine. The seeds are also good tossed in a salad, or over pickled beets.

Sweet Marjoram—(perennial)

Sweet marjoram is a mild-flavored bushy plant (2 feet high) that is easy to grow and can be used with many vegetables and entrees.

Nasturtium— (perennial)

Nasturtium is a vine with brightly colored flowers. The seeds, flowers, and leaves are all edible and have a peppery taste. Nasturtium seems to shoo away garden insects from the herb garden.

Oregano—(perennial)

Oregano is a hardy shrub-like plant (1 to 2 feet high) that thrives in the Bay Area. It is excellent in guacamole, spaghetti, pizza, and marinated salad. Oregano combines well with basil.

Parsley—(biennial)

Parsley is a bright green, compact plant (1 foot high) that enhances salads, vegetables, or entrees. It combines particularly well with garlic. Give parsley lots of water.

Rosemary—(perennial)

Rosemary is an attractive woody shrub that grows up to 2 to 6 feet high. There are both upright and trailing kinds. The leaves have a strong flavor. Rosemary is used traditionally in stuffings, or with chicken, lamb, and veal.

Sage—(perennial)

Sage is a gray-green shrub (1 to 2 feet high). It has a strong over-powering flavor that enhances fatty meats such as sausage or roast pork. Add it at the end of cooking or a camphor taste predominates.

Sorrel, or sourgrass—(perennial)

Sorrel (12 to 15 inches high), also called 'sourgrass,' looks like a weed. Sorrel leaves are chopped into salads, soups, or omelets. See March foods.

Spearmint—(perennial)

Spearmint is a lush green plant (1 to 2 feet high) that spreads rapidly (grow in a pot to restrain) and thrives on lots of water. It is used in teas, or chopped and added to peas or sauces for lamb and veal.

French tarragon—(perennial)

French tarragon is a dark green fragrant plant that is grown from a cutting (to 2 feet high). This strong-flavored herb is used in bearnaise sauce, green goddess dressing, or with fish and shellfish.

Thyme—(perennial)

Thyme is a hardy, spreading, bushy mat (5 inches high). This fragrant herb is very good with onions, carrots, beets, chicken, and fish.

April Foods

Arugula

Arugula—also called rocket, roquette, rugula—is a flat-leafed, coarse-textured herb (*Eruca sativa*) often used as a salad green. It has a nutty, somewhat peppery flavor. While it can be served alone, it is usually mixed with other salad greens—particularly 'Bibb' lettuce. Arugula can also be cooked; however it should be cooked briefly since cooking, even quickly, diminishes its unique pungent flavor. When cooked it combines well with garlic, tomatoes, and olives as well as other traditional Mediterranean foods. Arugula is sold by gourmet produce markets. It is easily grown from seed for either a spring or fall crop. As a member of the mustard family, arugula turns bitter as it ages—harvest or buy young leaves 3 to 5 inches long.

Salmon

Salmon is particularly good in April when it is caught in the Pacific ocean before it swims to fresh water streams to spawn—this early season salmon should be poached to preserve its flavor and texture. The finest tasting salmon is the King or Chinook—the largest of the species. It often weighs 25 pounds. Later in the year Silver salmon or Coho is caught—weighing 10 pounds, it is neither as rich nor as soft in texture as the King salmon. Pink salmon is the smallest, weighing 6 pounds, and is the most reasonably priced—not as rich tasting as King or Silver, its texture is fine and soft. Chum salmon is available in the fall and early winter—weighing 10 pounds, it is the least flavorful and it is improved by grilling over charcoal.

New Potatoes

Potatoes are planted continually throughout the year to be dug up at various times. Potatoes are grown in the foothills of the Sierra Nevada. In April, new potatoes are particularly small and delicious. Avoid potatoes with a greenish skin; they are often bitter tasting.

Parsley

Parsley blends well with most other herbs and has a natural affinity for garlic. Look for the red-skinned Mexican garlic, peel it and mash it with butter and lots of finely minced parsley. This simple sauce is excellent with new potatoes or red snapper, which is now coming to market from the Gulf Coast.

Bay Area Bakeries

Bakeries offer special breads for Easter. Listed here are some specialties sold by Bay Area establishments throughout the year as well as for Easter. The ethnic diversity of Bay Area bakeries offers a cultural as well as a culinary experience. Addresses for a variety of them are listed in the Ready Reference—Foods (bakeries).

Breads Sold at Easter

Panettone is an Italian yeast bread with raisins and candied fruit sold in many Bay Area supermarkets during the Christmas and Easter holidays. It is available throughout the year from Italian bakeries.

Vasilopita is a braided Greek Easter bread.

Kulich is a tall, cone-shaped Russian Easter bread, served usually with cheesy pashka.

Hot cross buns are one of the most familiar Easter season breads. Each yeast roll is filled with candied fruit and decorated with a glazed cross. Hot cross buns orginated in Great Britain where they are traditionally eaten on Good Friday.

Breads Sold All Year

Sourdough. A particular yeast strain gives sourdough bread its characteristic sour tangy flavor. Since the bread's arrival via gold miners, San Francisco's sourdough bread has been unique. Its special qualities are reputed to come from the old brick ovens or the moisture content of bay air, but it is just as likely to be the experience and care some bakeries put into their bread.

Italian. Italian bakeries and delicatessens sell a wide variety of breads. *Buccellato* is a ring shaped loaf made with raisins and anise. *Focaccia* is a flat bread which can taste sweet with raisins, or taste spicy when topped by chopped scallions or smothered in pizza sauce. There are also crunchy bread products such as the bread sticks called *grissini* or the many varieties of dried bread rectangles called *biscotti* which are perfect for dunking in your morning coffee.

Mexican. Tortillerias and Mexican delicatessens sell fresh flour and corn tortillas. A *tortilla* is a flat, unleavened pancake-like bread made with *masa harina* (ground corn). Look for the thick hand-patted *tortillas*. Mexican bakeries also sell a variety of *pan dulces* (sweet breads) and thick cookies.

April Celebrations

Landscape Garden Show—San Francisco

The San Francisco Landscape Garden Show presents an array of garden designs by professional landscape architects and designers. Twenty-five or thirty model gardens are displayed, from the whimsical to the dreamy to the practical. There are also talks and demonstrations by garden clubs and professionals.

Fisherman's Festival—Bodega Bay

The Fisherman's Festival is the annual celebration of the fishing community in Bodega Bay. There is a boat parade, blessing of the fleet, and an arts and crafts fair.

Strybing Arboretum Plant Sale—San Francisco

The annual plant sale in April (or May), sponsored by the Strybing Arboretum Society, is one of the largest plant sales in California. Customers have been known to line up for hours before the gates open to buy the rare and unusual plants. In addition to plants propagated from the Strybing Arboretum collection, many nurseries supply plants to be sold. There are smaller plant sales throughout the year at Strybing Arboretum.

Tilden Park Botanical Garden Sale—Berkeley

The Tilden Park Botanic Garden, located in Tilden Park not far from the Brazil Room, specializes in native Californian plants. On the third or fourth Saturday in April hundreds of plants propagated from the garden are sold. Come early and bring a box.

Wildflower Shows—various locations

In April many wildflowers bloom, and shows displaying hundreds of species of wildflowers are staged in many Northern California areas. Check the following institutions for the precise time of their wildflower shows. The Native Plant Society hosts a large show at the Oakland Museum in April or May. The annual Monterey Peninsula Wildflower Show is held at the Pacific Grove Museum of Natural History. There is a Spring Blossom and Wildflower Show in Golden Gate Park's County Fair Building.

Cherry Blossom Festival—San Francisco

Each spring, usually in April, the Japan Center hosts the Cherry Blossom Festival (Sakura Matsuri). The week-long festival includes martial arts, tea ceremonies, flower arranging, Japanese music and dance, films on Japan, bonsai exhibits, an Akita dog show, and several food bazaars. The most popular event is the grand parade which consists of over 1000 dancers, plus musicians, floats, and the popular sake barrel shrine. Most of the events are free.

Rodeos—Northern California

California holds more rodeos than any other state except Texas. Rodeos consist of a wide variety of spectator events, such as bareback and saddle bronc riding, bull riding, calf and team roping, steer wrestling, rodeo clowns called bull fighters who entertain as they save fallen cowboys from injury by drawing away bulls, calf decorating, wild cow milking, wild horse racing, mare and foal race, and horse show and trick riding.

Major Northern California rodeos are held in:
Red Bluff in April
Angels Camp in May
Livermore in June
and the biggest one in Salinas in July.

Opening Day of the Yachting Season—San Francisco Bay

The opening day of the yachting season is a festive boating event. It includes a procession (some boats are decorated, many fly colorful flags) past the St. Francis Yacht Club in San Francisco. Non-boaters can easily view boats from the breakwater frontage near the Marina Green in San Francisco. Another fine vantage point is Angel Island, where many boats anchor.

Good Old Days Celebration—Pacific Grove

The past is celebrated with two days of arts, crafts, food and entertainment in Pacific Grove. Simultaneously there is an annual Victorian House Tour and an annual Quilt Show.

Remember the days or month of an event may change. Consult the Ready Reference—Celebrations & Outings for details.

April

Wildflowers & Redwoods

April is an excellent month to walk in the uncrowded redwood forests admiring both the trees and the spring wildflowers. Several of the most common spring wildflowers found growing in redwood forests are illustrated on pages 55 and 56. Several of the most convenient redwood forests—from the Santa Cruz mountains to the coastal areas bordering Mount Tamalpais—are discussed here and on page 57.

The redwoods, *Sequoia sempervirens*, are among the oldest living things on earth—some of them are believed to be over 2,000 years old. They grow to a towering height of over 300 feet with a trunk diameter of up to 25 feet. Redwood trees grow only in a limited area of coastal California and southern Oregon.

Big Basin Redwoods State Park

Big Basin was the first state redwood park established by the state (1902). This 14,000-acre park is one of the most visited parks in California. It is located off Highway 236 which joins Highway 9 (from Saratoga to Santa Cruz). It contains fine groves of redwoods; some of which are as much as 330 feet tall and 18 feet in diameter.

There are also 40 miles of hiking trails, a natural history museum (with exhibits of local animals and plants), a post office, a campfire center, and several streams. There are 236 campsites but the campsites may still be closed in April; to find out phone the telephone number listed in the Ready Reference—Celebrations and Outings (Big Basin Redwoods State Park).

Henry Cowell Redwood State Park

A little further down Highway 9, going south from Felton, is the 4,072-acre Henry Cowell Redwood park. There are several nature trails here. One of the trails, near the picnic area, makes a one-mile loop through a grove of especially fine redwood trees. These trees are keyed to a printed commentary about them. One of the redwood trees, called the Giant Tree, is 51 feet in circumference, and 285 feet high.

There are also trails down to the San Lorenzo river which should be full in April. There are 105 campsites but they will probably be closed in April.

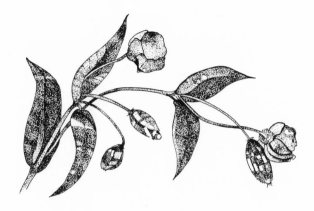

Fairy Lantern

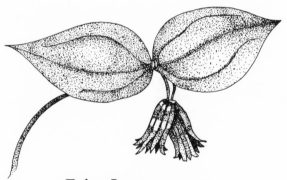

Fairy Lantern

Fairy lanterns (*Calochortus albus*) are delicate native wildflowers seen in the coastal range and in the Sierra foothills. They grow in shaded areas in woods and canyons. They are part of a large group of wildflowers known as mariposa lilies. The bulbs of certain mariposa-lilies were a source of food for California Indians.

Pacific Coast irises are illustrated on the April cover page. They are found on banks, grassy slopes, and open spaces in woodland areas. The colors of the flowers range from white to yellow to lavender or purple.

April Outings

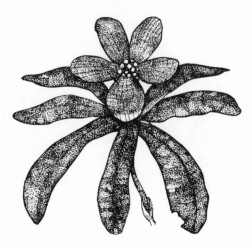

Stream Violet

Redwood Sorrel

Stream violet (*Viola sheltonii*). While the flower of a stream violet resembles the sweet violet of cultivated gardens, the sword-shaped leaves are distinctly different from the familiar heart-shaped leaves of the sweet violet. Many violet species grow in California in a variety of colors and leaf shapes.

Redwood sorrel (*Oxalis oregana*) is lush with clover-like leaves and pinkish flowers often veined with purple. It is native to coastal forests. A cousin, wood-sorrel (*Oxalis acetosella*), is one of several plants called shamrock.

Roaring Camp and Big Trees Narrow-Gauge Railroad

Just south of Felton is the picturesque Roaring Camp station. Here you can purchase tickets for a 6-mile train journey into the redwoods of the Santa Cruz mountains. The train is a steam engine built in 1880. The trip lasts 1 hour and 15 minutes. It stops briefly at a circular grove of towering redwoods called Cathedral Grove. The conductor narrates the history of the area during the trip.

It is possible to disembark at Bear Mountain during the train trip and hike or picnic for an hour or two before catching the train back. A short path connects Roaring Camp with Henry Cowell State Park. The park contains a circular walking tour of a spectacular grove of redwood trees. The tour is self-guided—an inexpensive guide sheet is sold at the park's gift shop.

See the Ready Reference—Celebrations & Outings (Roaring Camp) for more details.

Muir Woods National Monument

Situated 17 miles northwest of San Francisco on the slopes of Mt. Tamalpais, the 550-acre Muir Woods National Monument is easily accessible. The redwood groves are beautiful and impressive, but no camping or even picnicking is permitted.

Samuel P. Taylor State Park

Located a little farther north of Muir Woods is the 2,576-acre Samuel P. Taylor State Park. It is possible to picnic and camp among the park's second-growth redwoods. There are also hiking and bridle trails. In more accommodating weather, it is also possible to swim and wade in Lagunitas Creek.

Redwoods to the North

Some of the best-known redwood forests are much farther north in the Redwood National Park near the Oregon border. Designated as a UNESCO World Heritage Site, the park is acknowledged as "significant to other nations." Located here (after a 1.3-mile hike) is one of the world's tallest known trees—a 367.8-foot high redwood.

Redwood National Park incorporates private land as well as Jedediah Smith Redwood Park, Del Norte Coast Redwoods State Park, and Prairie Creek Redwoods State Park.

April Outings

Gold Country Wildflowers

April is a fine month to visit the gold-mining towns strung along Highway 49 in the foothills of the Sierra Nevada. At this time of year the hills are covered with lush green grass and the wildflowers are in bloom. Some wildflowers commonly found in the foothills of the Sierra Nevada are illustrated on pages 59 and 60.

The Gold Country is near enough to be a day trip and fascinating enough to spend several days touring from town to town. If you choose to spend the night, be sure to make reservations in one of the charming old inns. The towns are listed in the order you encounter them when driving on Highway 29 from Sonora to Nevada City. The entire trip is too tiring and hurried for a day trip; it is better to visit one major town or several nearby towns each day.

Sonora is a bustling, small town geared to the convenience of residents not tourists. St. James Episcopal church (1860) is a graceful example of Gold Country architecture. Sonora is the county seat of Tuolume County. There is a small county museum.

Jamestown is located near Sonora. It is a small town with antique shops, and a commercial development called Railtown 1897. Railtown offers tours of antique trains for a fee.

Columbia State Historic Park. Twelve square blocks of Columbia have been restored to recreate the Gold Rush era in its heyday. There is a blacksmith shop, a school house, a barbershop, saloons, and an old-fashioned candy kitchen with homemade candies. The restored Fallon Theater has stage shows evenings (except Monday) and Sunday afternoons. There is also a museum which presents free slide shows on Columbia's history. In the summer, there are stagecoach rides. The City Hotel (1856) is a state-run hostelry whose staff is aided by students from the Columbia Junior College Hospitality Management program. No automobiles are allowed in the park.

Angels Camp. Mark Twain had a cabin on nearby Jackass Hill; while visiting Angels Camp he heard a story from which he fashioned his famous short story, "The Celebrated Jumping Frog of Calaveras County." A Jumping Frog Jubilee is held each May (see May celebrations). Visit Angels Camp Museum to see the old buggies and wagons. White water raft trips on the Stanislaus and American rivers are available here.

More Gold Country towns are described on page 61.

Yerba Santa

Yarrow

Yerba santa (*Eriodictyon californicum*) is a 6-foot shrub that spreads in large patches along banks and ridges of the Sierra foothills. The flowers are pinkish blue to an off-white. Once pioneers brewed yerba santa into a tea for asthma or the sniffles.

Yarrow is a common name for a large group of aromatic herbs. The one illustrated here has a flat woolly white head (*Achillea borealis californica*) and is found in the Sierra foothills and down the coast into southern California. Pioneers steeped the leaves in hot water to stanch the flow of blood from cuts and wounds. It is also used in potpourri.

April Outings

Poppy

Tidy Tips

   Poppy (*Eschscholzia californica*) is the state flower. It is easily recognized by its bright orange-yellow blossom. The form varies somewhat depending upon the climate; for example it is more compact as it nears the coast.

   Tidy tips (*Layia platyglossa*) is a flower with a bright yellow center surrounded by a white fringe. It is partial to meadows and grassy slopes.

Murphys (Highway 4) is a small town with several historic buildings, a hotel, a saloon, and a museum. Located nearby are Calaveras Big Trees State Park with giant sequoias and Mercer Caverns (admission is charged at both).

San Andreas is an old town noted for the Calaveras County Historical Museum and archives. Nearby on Mountain Ranch Road is Cave City cavern (admission is charged).

Mokelumne Hill is a small town known for the historic, once-luxurious Leger Hotel. There are also a few shops and galleries.

Jackson is a small town where the Amador County Museum is located. Nearby there are abandoned mines with interesting tailing wheels.

Volcano requires a side trip up Highway 88. It is almost a ghost town, containing only a few small shops and a hotel. Daffodil Hill is located close by with over 200 species of daffodils in bloom during March and April. The Indian Grinding Rock State Park Historical Monument with over 1000 mortar holes is also nearby.

Amador City and **Sutter Creek** are small towns close together. They contain a few antique shops, inns, restaurants, and the Amador Museum.

Placerville is a large town with several historical buildings, and a museum. There is also a park with a lighted mine shaft.

Coloma is a very small town with two historic inns which contain popular dining rooms. It is known for the Marshall Gold Discovery State Historic Park (admission is charged). The park contains Marshall's cabin (1860), a museum, and the reconstructed Sutter's Mill.

Auburn is a large town, with a historic old section and restored buildings from the Gold Rush Era. Placer County Historical Museum is also located here—with recreated Victorian rooms, and Indian, Chinese and mining artifacts.

Grass Valley is a large town containing the Empire Mine State Historic Park (367 miles of mining passageway), the North Star Museum, and the Pelton Mining Museum.

Nevada City is discussed in the October outings section page 145.

April Outings

Mt. Tamalpais

Mt. Tamalpais, affectionately known as Mt. Tam, is situated north of San Francisco in Marin County. From Mt. Tamalpais' lofty 2,650 foot summit it is possible to gaze at both the San Francisco Bay and the Pacific Ocean. There are special pleasures associated with visiting Mt. Tamalpais in the spring. Not only are the wildflowers in bloom, but the rains have swollen the streams making them tumble and roar. April also brings the challenge of mud and of cold that nips at your cheeks and fingertips. So dress warmly and wear sturdy shoes—or better yet, wear boots.

A Hiker's Mountain

Mt. Tamalpais is a hiker's mountain frequented by so many so long that the trails are clearly defined and profuse. Trail maps, information, and guides are available at the Mt. Tamalpais State Park headquarters (Pan Toll Ranger's Station) located on the Panoramic Highway where it meets Stinson Beach Highway and Southside Road. Several trails also begin at the Pan Toll Station.

Where to Hike

East Peak's Scenic Trail. The East Peak's Scenic Trail is so level and short that it is a walk rather than a hike. It takes less than a half hour to complete the loop which offers one of the most spectacular panoramic views in the Bay Area. Park in the parking lot of Tamalpais' East Peak on Ridgecrest Road. The Scenic Trail is well marked. For a greater challenge, (a three hour round-trip trek) hike up to the peak on the well-marked Throckmorton Trail which begins at Mountain Home Inn on the Panoramic Highway.

Steep Ravine Trail. The hike on Steep Ravine Trail is wondrous in April when winter storms swell Webb Creek to cataracts. Begin the hike at the Pan Toll Ranger Station's parking lot—take the trail marked "Steep Ravine." The well-maintained trail leads through redwoods and ferns. One of the most notable features of the hike is a wood ladder which lowers the hiker down the side of a huge boulder while water rushes and hisses nearby.

For more information consult the Ready Reference—Celebrations & Outings (Mt. Tamalpais State Park).

May

The Ubiquitous Pelargonium

May Gardening

In Bloom

Annuals: ageratum, pansy, early petunia, sweet William
Perennials: carnation, daylily, felicia, iris, and pelargonium
Shrubs: azalea, rhododendron, and rose
Vines: bougainvillea, clematis, and wisteria

May is an excellent month to take cuttings from azaleas, carnations, chysanthemums, dianthus, fuchsias, and pelargonium.

Weed; and destroy earwigs, slugs, and snails.

Thin fruits when they are as big as a dime. This produces larger fruit and results in less weight damage to limbs.

Mow lawns and do not forget to water. Warm-weather-loving Bermuda and dichondra lawns should be planted now.

Prune uneven or unshapely growth on hedges, shrubs, and vines. Cut out dead wood wherever you find it.

Fertilize

If you fertilized in March, apply a second application to lawns, landscape plants, and established annuals and perennials. Azaleas, camellias, and rhododendrons prefer acid-type fertilizer after blooming. Citrus prefer citrus fertilizer with iron. If you applied fertilizer in April, wait four weeks before feeding again. If you have not fertilized yet, start now. The type of fertilizer is not of critical importance. Despite a plant's preference, an all-purpose fertilizer, high in nitrogen, can be applied to everything.

Roses

Roses are blooming now. Pick off faded blossoms and always cut to a five-leaf stem. Fertilize when most of the current buds have bloomed and blast off aphids with a strong spray of water.

The major rose ailments are:

Rust appears as bright orange spores on the undersides of leaves.

Mildew is a grayish powdery coating on leaves.

Black spot appears as black spots on leaves fringed with yellow. It is the most serious ailment and it can defoliate the entire plant.

Good garden practices help control these ailments. Water early in the day, prune to open the plant to good air circulation, and pick up the diseased leaves.

In the Nursery Look for:

Annuals: ageratum, aster, semperflorens begonia, impatiens, lobelia, petunia, zinnia
Perennials: geranium, pelargonium, marguerite, and Shasta daisy
Container-grown trees and shrubs
Vines: bougainvillea, clematis, and passiflora
Summer vegetables
Herbs

This is a good month to buy and plant rhododendrons while they are in full bloom and dormant.

Sow seeds of summer flowers such as cosmos, marigold, and zinnia, which are all easy to grow from seed.

Nurseries are now well stocked with summer-blooming annuals and perennials. Annuals include: ageratum, aster, semperflorens begonia, cosmos, impatiens, marigold, penstemon gloxinioides, petunia, sweet alyssum, sweet William, verbena, and zinnia. Perennials include: felicia, geranium, marguerite, pelargonium, and Shasta daisy.

Summer Vegetables

Plant your vegetable garden. Sow seeds of bush bean, carrot, chard, corn, cucumber, melon, pumpkin, radish, and squash. Buy eggplant, pepper, and tomato plants which take months to mature to fruition. See the following pages for more information on growing vegetables.

The Ubiquitous Pelargonium

May is the big month for pelargoniums (see the May cover illustration). Most of the plants we know as geraniums are technically pelargoniums. Whatever their name, they are commonly loved for their easy-to-care-for natures and their profusion of flowers. A new plant is easy to start—push a tip cutting from a non-blooming stem into damp sand and presto! Their only fault—a hard freeze kills them to the core.

All pelargoniums do well in pots. The common pelargonium (*Pelargonium hortorum*) also thrives in flower beds. There are pelargoniums with large elegant flowers (*Pelargonium domesticum*) and others that trail over a wall like ivy (*Pelargonium peltatum*). All pelargoniums love sunshine and should be tip-pinched when young to make them bushy. Pick faded flowers to favor new blossoms.

May Gardening Extra

Tomatoes

The most commonly grown garden vegetable—the tomato—is really a fruit. There are a few rules which make growing tomatoes easy. The most important one is to pick the right variety to plant in your garden.

Generally Bay Area gardeners should avoid what are known as beefsteak tomatoes—these large tasty tomatoes thrive in humid eastern summers where nighttime temperatures are high. In the fog-dominated sections of the Bay Area they are miserable—these huge plants yield few tomatoes and those few late-arriving tomatoes are often malformed.

Tomato Diseases

Another problem in the Bay Area is the tomato plant's vulnerability to verticillium wilt, a disease common in Bay Area soil. Fortunately certain varieties are resistant.

Following the tomato's name look for these symbols:
V   means resistant to verticillium wilt
F   means resistant to fusarium wilt
N   means resistant to nematodes
VFN   means resistant to all three

Recommended Tomato Plants

'**Better Boy**' (VFN) is a very vigorous plant that usually grows 6 feet tall and can grow to 14 feet tall. The tomatoes are large, very tasty, and slice beautifully. It produces abundant fruit and bears tomatoes until the winter cold.

'**Early Girl**' (V) is a very popular, large plant. The tomatoes are small to medium with a wonderful spicy flavor. It can be counted on to produce abundantly. Best of all, it produces tomatoes earlier than most other varieties.

'**Floramerica**' (VF) is an award-winning plant growing only 3 to 5 feet tall. All the medium-size, mild-flavored tomatoes ripen about the same time—handy if you plan to can tomatoes.

'**Red Cherry**' is a vigorous, large plant that produces an abundance of small, pop-in-the-mouth size tomatoes. The flavor is somewhat sweet.

When choosing a plant, look for a bushy one, avoiding tall, leggy plants. All tomato plants need the support of wire cages or stakes.

Tomato Growing Techniques

① Dig a hole approximately 1-foot deep and 1-foot wide. Add a heaping shovel full of well-rotted manure or compost and mix in with soil already in hole (not the soil you dug out).

② Carefully (don't disturb the fragile roots) remove the tomato plant from its container and set it rather deeply in the hole. The soil line should come just below the first set of leaves which means you are burying part of the stem as well as the roots. Gently add the dug-out soil to fill the hole to ground level but don't pat down or, worse, stomp down the soil around the plant.

③ Push back dirt around the plant to make a circular bank, a watering ring.

④ Stake. There are several methods. Use one hefty six foot stake driven in near the plant, pruning the plant to one stem and tying it to the stake (resulting in earlier but fewer tomatoes) or place a tall 6-inch mesh wire cage over the plant or drive 4 or more stakes around the plant.

⑤ Water deeply, especially before tomatoes form.

⑥ Important! wherever a leaf branch joins the stem another little stem forms. When these little stems form two or more leaves, pinch them out. Leave one or two if you want a multi-stemmed plant.

⑦ You can use a hormone spray to help blossoms set fruit. Tapping blossoms also seems to help.

⑧ Break off bottom branches to let the sun warm the soil around the plant.

Other Dependable Vegetables

Bush Beans are pretty and easy to grow. You can buy bush beans in six packs at the nursery. Set them 8 inches apart.

Cucumbers are relatively easy if you give them a wire mesh frame to grow on and plenty of sunshine and water. 'Spartan Valor' is a good choice for the Bay Area.

Radishes are easy. Poke a few seeds in any extra space. Try 'French Breakfast' or 'White Icicle' varieties.

Zucchini are easy if you have lots of sunshine and room (4 feet when mature). In foggy area they tend to mildew.

May Foods

Mangoes

Spicy, exotic-flavored mangoes begin their season in May. Look for plump, unblemished fruit with lots of rich yellow and red color. They are slightly soft when ripe.

Sugar Snap Peas

Look for sweet sugar snap peas. This newcomer is a cross between English peas and snow peas. They should be plump and vivid green.

Strawberries

Strawberries are at their peak in May. Tart field-grown rhubarb is also at its peak and combines well with strawberries in pies.

Onions

From May until fall there are more onion varieties—the most popular are discussed below. Markets sell several varieties simultaneously.

Bermuda onions are large, flat, delicately flavored onions. They are eaten raw in salads or sandwiches, but they are also good sauteed, and for deep-fried onion rings.

Chives are mild, decorative onions perfect for folding into omelets and sprinkling over food.

Globe onions are the common cooking onions available year round; they are usually yellow and have a strong flavor.

Italian onions are available year round but they are sweetest during this time. These purple-red onions are perfect for salads.

Leeks are grown locally. They are at their peak in May (and again in early fall). They are queen of the soup onions; they are also good braised. Wash out all the grit that lurks between the leaves.

Pearl onions are not a variety of onion but a specific size of onion. These tiny onions are good cooked or pickled.

Red torpedo onions are crisp, sweet, blimp-shaped onions that are available in early summer. They are great in salads and sandwiches.

Scallions are also called green onions. Use both the green top and white stem either raw or cooked.

Shallots are mild, distinctive, almost garlic-flavored onions which are divided into cloves. They are queen of the sauce onions and are at their best late summer and early fall. Never cook them until brown or they turn bitter.

Selecting Fish in the Bay Area

May's calm weather brings better fishing conditions resulting in an in-crease in fresh fish available in Bay Area markets. Fresh fish should smell like the sea. It should look moist and lustrous even when sliced. For the best flavor and texture fish should be cooked the same day it is caught. If you must use frozen fish avoid frozen fish that has been thawed before purchase. Ask for packages of fish still frozen. Also avoid fish basking in cloudy white liquid or with ice crystals which indicate dehydration. Use fish the day you buy it or while still frozen. As a fish dries out the gelatinous tissue breaks down, destroying flavor and texture.

Fish Available in the Bay Area

Ling cod is fished locally and is plentiful in good weather. It is also reasonably priced and tastes fine.

Halibut and **flounder** are flat, delicately flavored fish. The Pacific halibut is caught north of the Bay Area and is considered superior to California halibut.

Pacific red snapper is one of several delicious, red-skinned rockfish pulled from Pacific waters. Other rockfish to look for are the bolina, black, blue, and yellowtail rockfish.

Sablefish is also called butterfish or black cod. This rich, buttery, mild-flavored fish is perfect for barbecuing or grilling. Serve sablefish with a rich sauce.

Salmon are fished locally when they come into the bay to spawn. This distinctive, rich-tasting fish has several varieties; King salmon is the best and most expensive. See April Foods page 50 for more information on salmon.

Shark has a firm texture and a taste similar to swordfish which is more expensive. Locally thresher shark is often available.

Pacific sole are fished all year with abundant quantities available in the good weather months. These flat fish have a very delicate flavor and are low in fat so you should saute them very quickly. The filets are thin and flexible and can be easily rolled around fillings, such as crab or shrimp, and then poached.

Trout are available pond-raised from local and out-of-state sources. Many fish-market proprietors consider the pond-raised trout from Idaho to be the best.

May Celebrations

Botanical Sales—Bay Area

Several major botanical gardens hold large plant sales in May. This is an opportunity to buy rare and unusual plants. The University of California Botanical Garden in Berkeley holds its sale in May. Also check with the arboreta at U.C. Santa Cruz and U.C. Davis.

Saratoga Blossom Festival—Saratoga

The Saratoga festival revives a traditional celebration when people came by horse and buggy to see spring blossoms in Saratoga. In addition to flowers, the festival includes wine tasting, ethnic food booths, and arts and crafts.

Great Monterey Squid Festival—Monterey

One of the newer Bay Area festivals is the Monterey Squid Festival, which celebrates the local catch of this tasty cephalopod. The fair includes educational displays as well as food and music.

Cinco de Mayo—Bay Area

Parades, fiestas with mariachi music, costumed dancers, arts and crafts, and Mexican food booths are scheduled throughout the Bay Area during the week of May fifth.

In San Francisco there is usually a weekend parade.

In San Jose there is a celebration at the County Fairgrounds.

Dixieland Jubilee—Sacramento

The Jubilee is one of the largest jazz festivals anywhere. For four days, spanning Memorial Day weekend, bands play in the balconies, streets, and cabarets of Sacramento's charming and historic old town.

Bay to Breakers—San Francisco

The world's largest foot race is loved by viewers as well as racers. Some racers wear costumes or join hands while racing. Check the *San Francisco Examiner*, which sponsors the event, for details.

Charmarita—Half Moon Bay

Charmarita is a Portuguese festival dating back to Queen Isabella of Portugal. Half Moon Bay has celebrated Charmarita for over 100 years. There is a parade, a carnival, a barbecue and a dance.

Calaveras County Fair and Jumping Frog Jubilee

The Calaveras fair at Angels Camp includes livestock exhibits, a horse show, dancing, a kiddies' day parade, a lot of frog jumping, an air show, a destruction derby, a rodeo, and fireworks.

Berryessa Art and Wine Festival—San Jose

The Berryessa festival includes over 100 artists plus wine tasting, entertainment, and ethnic food on the second weekend in May.

Festival of the Sea—San Francisco

The Festival of the Sea is a celebration of San Francisco's nautical heritage. It includes shanty concerts, nautical poetry, tours of historical ships, and demonstrations of marine skills.

Russian River Wine Festival—Healdsburg

The Russian River festival is held in the town plaza. Over 30 local wineries participate. It includes arts, crafts, and entertainment.

Music at the Paul Masson Winery—Saratoga

The Paul Masson winery presents internationally known musicians in outdoor concerts at its mountain winery. Jazz and folk, and classical performances are held on alternate weekends. Late May to September. There is wine tasting during intermissions. Reservations are a must.

Greek Festivals—Bay Area

For many parishes of the Orthodox Greek Church, the Greek festival is the big social event of the year. In May there are celebrations of the Greek culture in Oakland, San Jose, and San Rafael.

Concours d' Elegance—Bay Area

Sanctioned by the Sports Car Club of America, with proceeds going to charity, a Concours d' Elegance is a display of carefully restored antique cars, retired racing cars, and imports. In late May or early June, there are concourses in Hillsborough and at the Silverado Country Club.

Remember the day, even the month, of an event may change from year to year. For more information consult the Ready Reference—Celebrations & Outings.

May Outings

Mendocino and Fort Bragg

May is a good month to drive to the coastal towns of Mendocino and Fort Bragg, which are located approximately 150 miles north of San Francisco. The rhododendrons and azaleas are in bloom in May and the thick fog bank has yet to make its daily trek inland.

Mendocino

The first glimpse of Mendocino is enchanting. The town is perched on the headland, which juts out into the north side of Mendocino Bay. Mendocino appears to be transplanted from the Eastern seaboard. It consists of white painted gothic houses with steep gabled roofs, stores with fake fronts, New England salt box houses, and a few boardwalks. The first glimpse of Mendocino seems so unlike California that you may blink involuntarily as if it were an illusion.

But no tricks are being played. As unlikely as it seems way up here in the middle of nowhere, Mendocino was, at the turn of the century, a thriving port city. It had 8 hotels and 21 saloons. This is a leftover town—when the logging played out and the trains sank the shipping industry, Mendocino dwindled until its rebirth as an artists' village.

Today its historical integrity is carefully preserved. There are a number of inns that offer cozy Victorian accommodations from tiny attic rooms to large, balconied rooms with sweeping ocean views. There are also restaurants as sophisticated as those in San Francisco.

Tranquil Pleasures

After sleeping and eating, try canoeing on the nearby river. Visitors typically rise late, breakfast, and then mosey down Main Street to watch the ducks swim in the pond across from the McCallum House, browse the craft shops, or read until time for lunch.

Highlights of a Mendocino visit include watching the sunset on the headlands. At the cliff edge you can hear the water howling down a wave tunnel and see the sun set in a mist of melancholy splendor. Then the lights go on in Mendocino and it is time for dinner.

Nearby are two luxurious resorts—the gilded Heritage House, and the subtly superb Little River Inn. Both are great places to dine or breakfast. You can also visit the Kelly Historical House or perhaps see a movie at the Art Center. There is also the option of visiting the Mendocino Coast Botanical Gardens or riding the Skunk Train.

Fort Bragg

Fort Bragg is located a few miles north of Mendocino. It is about as different from Mendocino as Salinas is from San Francisco. In 1857 it was really a fort built to oversee the coastal Indians on the 24,000-acre Mendocino Indian Reservation. Then lumbermen became interested in timber located near Fort Bragg and that was the end of both the fort and the Indian reservation.

Today Fort Bragg looks like a lumber company town. It is a workers' community—busy, thriving, and complete with drive-in hamburger stands. Not that Fort Bragg is without charm. Noyo Harbor (within Fort Bragg city limits) with its commercial fishing boats is a totally authentic fishermen's domain. It has a rough appeal based on its practical buildings and busy piers.

Most of the lodgings in Fort Bragg are motels which emphasize convenience rather than charm. But there are also a handful of picturesque and historic inns.

California Western Railroad (Skunk Train)

The railroad line between Fort Bragg and Willits was completed in 1911. The term "skunk train" was invented in 1925 when the first diesel engines replaced the cleaner smelling steam engines. Today this scenic railroad is so popular that reservations are almost always necessary. The trip through the redwood forest includes two tunnels and many bridges.

Mendocino Coast Botanical Gardens

After paying an entrance fee, the visitor may meander over well-marked paths through 47 acres of lush woods and meadows. The rhododendrons are spectacular in May and so is the view of the rugged coastline.

Camping

Campers are in luck. There are few coastal campgrounds in Northern California but two are situated here—Van Damme State Park and Russian Gulch State Park. Both parks are very pretty and have forest trails as well as beach front areas.

Consult the Ready Reference—Celebrations & Outings (Fort Bragg, Mendocino) for more information.

May Outings

Wondrous Yosemite

Yosemite National Park is located approximately 200 miles east of the Bay Area, (about a 5-hour drive). It is one of the most outstanding scenic attractions in the United States. May is a good month to visit Yosemite because the falls are full from melting snow, and the tourist season is not at its height.

Yosemite Valley can make an adult a child again—full of a child's sense of wonder and awe. You behold the muted silver-grays of this glacial gorge of sheer rock walls. You inhale the rich, forest scent of pines and firs. You feel the crisp air nip your cheeks and finger tips. And walking up the broad path toward lower Yosemite Falls, you hear the muted roar of the falls swelling louder until up close it deafens you to every other sound.

At night, tucked in against the cold, you may hear again the roar of Yosemite Falls and once again the muted colors of the valley may play upon your closed eyelids. Yosemite has that kind of impact.

Scenic Attractions in the Valley

Yosemite Falls. In May, lower Yosemite Fall is truly spectacular. The walk up the broad, one-third-mile-long path has many impressive views of the falls. The lower waterfall alone is more than twice the height of Niagara Falls—the height explains the thunderous roar you hear when standing close by.

Other scenic valley features include **Bridalveil Falls** and **Vernal Falls**. There are also the massive rock formations named Half Dome, El Capitan, Sentinel Rock, The Three Brothers, and Cathedral Rocks. They change with shifting sunlight, shadows, and moonlight.

Scenic Attractions Outside the Valley

Glacier Point provides an impressive view of both the valley and the Sierra Nevada. It is reached by car or by a long, strenuous but worthwhile hike.

Mariposa Grove. A 35-mile drive leads to the giant sequoias of Mariposa Grove. On the same trip it is convenient to visit the Pioneer Yosemite History Center at Wawona.

Tuolumne Meadows. A scenic drive on the Tioga Road leads into high country and to Tuolumne Meadows. Tuolumne Meadows is the highest sub-alpine meadow in the high Sierra.

Yosemite Village

The Visitor Center at Yosemite Village has displays and audio-visual programs pertaining to the valley. There is a very good nature program which offers hikes, walks, lectures, and special-interest tours. Nearby the Indian Cultural Museum has interesting displays of Miwok and Paiute history. Also in the village are several shops; one of them sells Indian crafts; another shop sells Ansel Adam prints.

Dining

There are delicatessens, grocery stores, cafeterias, and restaurants in Yosemite Valley. The Ahwahnee Hotel is the outstanding place to dine— the immense dining room is both elegant and rustic with thick timber beams, chandeliers, and three-story windows framing majestic views. Go for breakfast, if you can not get dinner reservations.

Accommodations in the Valley

Curry Village may be the most fun place to stay. It is rustic and funky with a choice of tent cabins or redwood cabins.

Yosemite Lodge has modern hotel and motel type rooms. Older cabins are also available with or without baths.

The Ahwahnee Hotel is the best place to stay in the valley. It is impressive, elegant, and expensive. But, go forewarned! Reservations are difficult to get, and ties for men are required for dinner.

Camping is available in several valley campgrounds. It is limited to a seven-day stay. Reservations can be made through Ticketron.

Outside the Valley

The Wawona Hotel is a charming, old-fashioned hotel near Mariposa Grove. As charming as this hotel is, staying there is not as pleasant as being in the valley.

High Sierra Camps. Hikers and horseback riders can enjoy these camps where dormitory beds and tents are clustered near a central dining area (family-style dining).

Camping is available at the more than 1,000 campsites outside the valley. Campers are limited to a 14-day stay.

Make reservations early. Consult the Ready Reference—Celebrations & Outings (Yosemite) for details.

May Outings

Audubon Canyon Ranch

Audubon Canyon Ranch is a wildlife sanctuary located in Marin County on Shoreline Highway, three miles north of Stinson Beach. Over 90 species of land birds may be observed there, although the main attraction is the heronry of the great blue herons and great egrets. May is an excellent month for visiting Audubon Canyon Ranch because the wildflowers are still in bloom and the rookery is full of young birds.

Herons and Egrets

The great blue heron is the largest heron in North America. It stands four feet to five feet tall, with a wing span of nearly six feet. The American egret is smaller, with a wing span of about four and one-half feet. Several months ago these majestic birds will have come to Audubon Canyon Ranch to court and nest. Two to five eggs are laid in each nest and are incubated by both parents for about 28 days. One to five offspring survive to take flight.

Schwarz Grove Rookery

As you walk toward the Schwarz Grove Rookery the bird cries grow louder, a sound that heightens your anticipation and quickens your pace. But it does not prepare you. At last you look out across the canyon and see, perhaps with a feeling of astonishment, the flattened tops of tall redwoods where over 200 great egrets and great blue herons have made large nests of sticks.

This sight is a little overwhelming. Fortunately there is usually a naturalist at Henderson Overlook to explain the natural phenomena of the heronry. Telescopes are available for closer viewing.

The Facilities

The Audubon Canyon Ranch is open only from March 1 to July 4. Admission is free. Visitors are asked to register upon arrival. There is no entrance fee. Contributions are welcome.

A display hall introduces visitors to Audubon Canyon Ranch. The ranch has several trails, a picnic area, and a bookstore.

It is a good idea to bring binoculars.

For more information consult the Ready Reference—Celebrations & Outings (Audubon Canyon Ranch).

The Variable Season

Temperature—cool to warm
    mid fifties to mid seventies

The coldest winter I ever spent was a summer in San Francisco.
Attributed to Mark Twain

The hot Central Valley inhales the cooler ocean air through drafts created in mountain gaps. On its way to the Central Valley the cool ocean air pulls a high blanketing layer of fog over the Bay Area. This sun-shielding fog gives the Bay Area a reputation for cool, overcast summers. But it does not always happen. Some summers are practically fogless. And even in our foggiest summers, there are a few bright sunny days. The complex weather elements are unpredictable.

The Pacific High, a mass of cool, heavy air about a thousand miles offshore, usually blocks summer rain storms from entering the Bay Area. The only form of precipitation during the summer is the fog. Amazingly the fog drip can amount to 10 inches annually, enough to support groves of redwoods and pines.

Summer Outings

The high summer fog cycles in and out of existence, giving us sunny days among overcast ones. On cool, cloudy days it is easy to drive out of Bay Area weather. The Sacramento Delta is usually hot and sunny, perfect for July picnics. Swimmers can seek out Stinson Beach and Tomales Bay, which are often shielded from wind and fog by the projecting mass of Point Reyes Peninsula. The Russian River is also a favorite of summer swimmers.

Foods and Gardening

This is the finest season for fresh fruits and vegetables. Because the Bay Area is well situated among fruit orchards, berry fields, and vegetable farms, it is possible to make a variety of trips to pick fresh produce. It is also the season to haul out the canning equipment and jam jars.

It is a pleasant though baffling season for Bay Area gardeners. A gardener can never accurately anticipate whether this is the summer to grow corn, melons, and zinnias or whether overcast weather will thwart the effort. During the variable season Bay Area gardens bloom with dependable plants such as fuchsia, hydrangea, impatiens, and lobelia.

Seasonal Reminders

In addition to the outings recommended for June, July, and August, the following phenomena provide alternative seasonal excursions.

Great Blue Herons and American Egrets

Great blue herons and great egrets nest at Audubon Canyon Ranch. See May outings page 76. The Audubon Canyon Ranch is open only from March 1 to July 4.

Stellar Sea Lions

Stellar sea lions arrive at Año Nuevo to mate during the late summer months. See February outings pages 24 to 27.

June

Red Raspberries

June Gardening

In Bloom

Annuals: ageratum, lobelia, petunia, sweet alyssum, and sweet William
Perennials: daylily, carnation, felicia, geranium, pelargonium and marguerite
Bulb-like: gladiolus, Japanese iris, and lily
Shrubs: fuchsia, hibiscus, hydrangea, and rose
Vines: bougainvillea, clematis, and star jasmine

By June, primroses finish their spring display of flowers. If you cut back their leaves (hold them up like rabbit ears) by one-third to one-half they will probably flower again mid-summer.

Pinch back chrysanthemums and marguerites.

Continue to pick off faded rhododendron flowers.

Fertilize roses. If they are a variety of climbing rose that blooms once a year, prune them when they finish flowering. The combination of an overcast sky and warm weather often causes a layer of powdery mildew to form. Water early in the day and plant roses in an area with good air circulation to reduce the mildew.

Fertilize lawns with lawn (high nitrogen) fertilizer. Fertilize azaleas, camellias, hydrangeas, and rhododendrons with an acid fertilizer. Fertilize everything else with an all-purpose fertilizer—especially blooming annuals and perennials.

Fuchsia and Hydrangea

Pinch back the tips of fuchsias. When watered and fertilized regularly, fuchsias bloom profusely throughout summer and fall. After fuchsia blossoms fall off, thick reddish-pink balls remain—remove them to promote flowering.

Hydrangeas are similar to fuchsias in their need for plenty of water; they wilt quickly without enough. A deep watering will soon revive either plant.

Sweet Alyssum and Lobelia

Sweet alyssum and lobelia are two profusely blooming, low-growing, spreading, mat-like plants. Both are easy to grow in the Bay Area and an excellent choice to cover the soil of potted plants or to fill in a flower bed. The most common variety of sweet alyssum has tiny, white, speck-like flowers with a honey-like fragrance. Lobelia comes in several colors; all have delicate, cascading flowers.

In the Nursery Look for:

Annuals: impatiens, marigold, and petunia
Perennials: agapanthus, daylily, geranium, and marguerite
Shrubs: fuchsia, hibiscus, and hydrangea
Summer vegetables

Set out container-grown plants as long as the weather is not too hot. If the weather is hot, wait until evening to plant, and rig temporary shade to shield plants for several days.

There is still time to put in a summer vegetable garden. From seeds, you can grow bean, carrot, chard, and radish. From nursery transplants, you can grow corn, cucumber, eggplant, melon, pepper, squash, and tomato. Do not delay any further with your vegetable garden. Many plants require several months to mature.

Flowering Drought-Tolerant Plants

There are many plants from dry-summer, wet-winter areas similar to our own that, once established, grow here with little or no supplemental water. The following drought-tolerant plants offer attractive year-round form and seasonal flowers.

African daisy (*Arctotis hybrids*) forms a flowering mound about ten inches high and three feet wide. The flowers come in many colors and bloom in spring and early summer, with sporadic bloom throughout the year.

Fleabane (*Erigeron karvinskianus*) is a low-growing tangle of narrow leaves and fringed white (tinged pink) daisies. It can be used in hanging baskets.

Fortnight lily (*Dietes vegeta*) is a three-foot-high plant with narrow, iris-like leaves and open, waxy, white flowers blotched gaily with a touch of yellow-orange.

Golden shrub daisy (*Euryops pectinatus*) is a three-foot rounded shrub that is covered with bright yellow daisies in spring, summer, and fall.

Gray lavender cotton (*Santolina chamaecyparissus 'Compacta'*) is a neat two-foot, rounded, gray-green shrub with yellow button flowers in summer.

Mexican sage (*Salvia leucantha*) is a gray-green shrub with long, velvety, purple spikes that reach dramatically for the sun.

Sea lavender (*Limonium perezii*) is best known for its paper-like blooms (usually purple), which are sold as dried flowers. It is attractive all year with its wavy clump of dark green leaves topped by a large (up to two feet tall) spray of flowers. Do not overwater.

June Foods

Apricots

Almost all commercially grown apricots come from California and are harvested from May through August. June and July are considered the best months for buying them. Look for a rich, golden-orange color that indicates tree-ripened maturity. Avoid those with greenish casts. A ripe apricot is slightly soft.

Bing Cherries

When selecting Bing cherries look for a dark-red color, plump and glossy-looking skins, and perky, fresh-looking stems. They are a delicate fruit and should be handled carefully. The Bing cherry is a fresh eating cherry; pies are made out of tart cherries usually only found canned, such as the Montmorency cherry.

Haricots Verts

Haricots verts are small, slender green beans known by their French name. With a wonderful intense flavor and crisp texture, they may be steamed, sauteed, or boiled. Lightly steamed, they are an attractive addition to salads. Haricots verts are available from gourmet produce markets.

Lemongrass

Lemongrass is not a seasonal food but it is so new to most Bay Area cooks that it is included here. Lemongrass is an aromatic tropical grass with a pungent lemon taste that is widely used in Southeast Asian cookery. It is available in some Bay Area produce markets and many Asian groceries, particularly Thai and Vietnamese markets. There are several ways to use lemongrass. One method is to finely slice the stalk and add it to a strongly flavored dish such as a curry. Another method is to bruise (but not slice) either the entire stalk or a smaller section of it and add it to a marinade, sauce, or soup. The tops can be dried and brewed into a tea. If you can obtain a root of lemongrass it is easy to grow in Bay Area gardens.

Radishes

Radishes are at their peak in June. In addition to using them in salads (you might include a bit of their green tops as the French do), grate them into cream cheese to spread over pumpernickle bread.

Berries

June is the big berry month—all the berries (except cranberries) are in season.

Blueberries are not a California berry although they are occasionally sold fresh in Bay Area markets. Look for plump berries with a silvery, powdery coating. They are very perishable—use promptly.

Boysenberries are grown mainly in California. This delicious, tart berry is unsurpassed for pies. Watch out for mold and do not wash or core boysenberries until you are ready to use them.

Ollalieberries are locally grown and similar to, but not as sweet as, boysenberries. When buying ollalieberries look for a truly black color for the best taste.

Raspberries are locally grown. They are often considered the queen of the berries. This is the only berry whose core is pulled out at picking. Without a core, they are more perishable, and therefore more expensive. Avoid raspberries with any green cells—they are not ripe.

Strawberries are locally grown. Look for firm, fully ripe berries. Peek underneath the basket to be sure they are not moldy.

Strawberry Jam

The best strawberry jam is made without added pectin, but gauging the pectin content of fresh fruit is tricky. To assure a high natural pectin content use berries promptly after picking them or choose one-fourth of the strawberries with a green cast.

Freezer Jam

If sterilizing glasses over a hot stove is too much work, consider freezer jam made with liquid pectin. This uncooked jam is extraordinarily easy to make and has a wonderful fresh fruit taste. The disadvantage is the high proportion of sugar liquid pectin requires.

Freezing Berries

Freezing berries for later use in pies, tarts, and preserves is easy. The texture is changed and they tend to weep a little when thawed, but the flavor is good. All the berries except blueberries can be washed, hulled and combined with three-fourths of a cup of sugar for every quart of berries and then packed into containers and frozen. Blueberries should be steamed one minute and frozen with no sugar added.

June Celebrations

North Beach Fair—San Francisco

San Francisco's oldest street fair occurs on Father's Day weekend with 200 artists and craftspeople on Grant Avenue from Vallejo to Filbert. Excellent Italian food is combined with rhythm-and-blues music and lots of arts and crafts booths.

Street Performers Festival—San Francisco

The Street Performers Festival, featuring performances by musicians, mimes, jugglers, and other street artists, is held at Pier 39.

Festival at the Lake—Oakland

Lake Merritt provides a calm backdrop for the enormous two-day festival which features a very large selection of foods, arts, and music spread out over several areas of the park so it does not seem crowded.

Gay Freedom Day Parade—San Francisco

The parade consists of floats, bands, and thousands of participants who march down Market Street from Spear to Civic Center Plaza where the celebration continues with arts, crafts, games and food booths.

Wine Festival—Mill Valley

On the last weekend in June over 50 vintners and the Rouge et Noir Cheese Company participate in the Mill Valley Wine Festival.

Menlo Town Fair—Menlo Park

The fair has arts, crafts, and entertainment—first Sunday in June.

San Francisco Art Festival—San Francisco

The San Francisco Art Festival is one of the oldest art shows in the Bay Area. It includes arts, crafts, and entertainment.

Sunnyvale Arts & Wine Festival—Sunnyvale

On the second weekend in June, over 225 artists and craftspersons plus Santa Clara vintners participate in the Sunnyvale festival.

Union Street Spring Fair—San Francisco

In front of Union Street's Victorian buildings there are over 300 arts and crafts booths from Gough to Fillmore—the Union Street Spring Fair includes special events such as a Waiter's Race and Tea Dancing.

San Francisco Summer Festival—San Francisco

The Summer Festival is a two-month series of events using the city's opera, symphony, and ballet, plus about 150 local sources of talent.

Golden Gate Park Band Shell—San Francisco

There are often free weekend summer performances beginning about noon at the music concourse in Golden Gate Park.

Municipal Band Concerts—Oakland

Free concerts are held at Lake Merritt's bandstand—Sunday afternoons.

Spring Folk Music Festival—San Francisco

Everyone can participate in the folk singing and dancing sponsored by the San Francisco Folk Music Club, free, at Fort Mason.

Midsummer Music Festival—San Francisco

The music festival is a free outdoor concert series in Stern Grove's natural amphitheater. The 2 P.M. June to August Sunday concerts may include the San Francisco Opera, Symphony, and Ballet as well as renowned musicians in jazz, pop, and Dixieland—arrive early.

Music at Montalvo—Saratoga

Classical, contemporary, and chamber music is performed outdoors at the Villa Montalvo Center for the Arts—wine tasting at intermissions.

Summer Music Festival—Rutherford

Jazz concerts are performed under the stars at the Robert Mondavi Winery during the Summer Music Festival—June through July.

Russian River Country Music Festival—Guerneville

The festival's music concerts are held outdoors at Johnson's Beach; bring a picnic, blanket, and perhaps a bathing suit.

Art and Wine Festival—Novato

The festival is usually held the last weekend in June in old-town. Several wineries participate—there are many arts and crafts booths.

Remember the days, even the months, of events may change. Consult the Ready Reference—Celebrations & Outings for details.

June Outings

Incredible Mt. Lassen

Mt. Lassen is located 250 miles north of the Bay Area where the Cascades join the Sierra Nevada. Although Mt. Lassen is California's smallest national park, its impact on the visitor is large. June is about as early in the year as possible to visit Mt. Lassen. It is snowy during the winter and thus is perfect for tranquil cross-country skiing.

Volcano

Once Mt. Lassen was considered just another mountain—a landmark named after a pioneer emigrant. Then on May 30, 1914, it came suddenly to life. It belched and spit until nearly a year later it blew its top off, bursting open the mountain, spilling molten lava, and destroying everything in its path for miles. Ashes settled as far away as Reno, Nevada, where they covered the roads several inches deep. The volcanic eruptions continued until 1917.

Today Mt. Lassen is a visual reminder of the destructive force that lurks below ground. It has a haunting and unearthly appearance—it is a little like visiting another planet.

What to See

It is possible to drive through Mt. Lassen Volcanic Park in a little over an hour, but at least a day is needed to realize the wonders of Mt. Lassen. It is a park to experience with all your senses. Visually it is stunning, but it also assaults your sense of smell and touch. The following are areas to visit.

Bumpass Hell Trail

The most spectacular of Mt. Lassen's hydrothermal areas is reached by a trail called Bumpass Hell Trail which descends into a basin eaten away by acids. In the basin Mother Nature provides quite a show. The ground hisses from steam vents, water boils in pools, and mud pots gurgle in a real life scene from a late night horror show. The hot spring, Old Steam Engine, erupts in a gushing roar to shroud everything in a white mist. In one area of the basin deep turquoise waters shimmer above a layer of fool's gold. With a sense of relief you may well end up hurrying the 1.3 miles back to the sane world where you parked your car.

Chaos Crags and Chaos Jumbles

Chaos Crags are hardened pink lava plugs pushed up from the earth over a thousand years ago. Chaos Jumbles are rock-slides caused by steam explosions. Some of the twisted little conifers in Chaos Jumbles (known as the Dwarf Forest) are 250 years old.

Cinder Cone

A pretty trail, 1½ miles long, leads to Cinder Cone. It is a peculiar looking mountain of black granular cinder rising 700 feet. Climbing Cinder Cone is like climbing a sand dune of crushed coal. From the top you can take another trail down into the crater.

Devastated Area

The molten hot eruption of 1915 stripped all vegetation from the Devastated Area and it is now going through natural reforestation. Near the north end of Devastated Area there is Hot Rock—a huge black lava rock carried down from Lassen Peak by the mud flow of 1915.

Sulphur Works Thermal Area

Sulphur Works Thermal Area is a miniature Bumpass Hell with steam vents, boiling hot springs, and bubbling mud pots. You are correctly warned to stay on the trail; a false step could be catastrophic.

Summit Lake

Summit Lake is a pretty lake which is popular with swimmers and campers. Rangers give campfire programs in the summer.

Boiling Springs Lake

A two-mile nature trail leads around the Boiling Springs Lake and across a meadow and through a pretty forest. True to its name, the lake bubbles and boils.

Where to Stay

Mt. Lassen is a camper's park and accommodations are limited. Make reservations well ahead of your visit if you wish to stay at either Manzanita Lake Lodge (dining room, cabins, and cottages) or at Drakesbad Guest Ranch (limited accommodations, dining room).

See the Ready Reference—Celebrations & Outings for details.

June Outings

Picking Your Own Produce

In the greater Bay Area there are many farmers who sell produce direct from the growing fields. Each seasonal harvest produces its own interesting experience. For example, strawberry picking in June usually means squatting down between long furrows of strawberry plants with muddy knees and red-stained fingertips. When the strawberry picking is done near Watsonville, it is easy to combine the outing with a trip to a nearby beach in Santa Cruz (see the last June Outing). One of the joys of picking your own produce is that each area of harvest can be combined with a scenic excursion. Harvesting corn in July around Brentwood can be combined with a trip through the nearby Delta (see July Outings). Later in the year, apple picking in October combines well with a trip to the Sierra foothills (see October Outings).

Where to Pick Produce

Several excellent, free guides to the regions in the Bay Area where produce is sold directly to the public are listed in the Ready Reference— Celebrations and Outings under harvest guides. Write for them and enclose a large self-addressed stamped envelope with each request. The guides usually include a harvest map.

How to Prepare

All the guides recommend phoning the farmer or rancher to make certain the harvest is ripe and the farm open for business.

Although many places have already-picked produce available, it is more fun and cheaper to pick it yourself.

Bring boxes, baskets, sacks. Most produce is sold by the pound.

June Harvest

At the top of the list for picking in June are the berries: strawberries, boysenberries, ollalieberries, and some red currants. (Raspberries are picked later.) Berries grow in many different parts of the Bay Area—one of the best known is just outside of Watsonville, between Santa Cruz and Monterey. Route 152 traverses much of this area from Highway 1 up to Hecker Pass in the Santa Cruz mountains.

Also ready for harvest in June are apricots, the last of the locally grown cherries, and early peaches.

Bay Area Harvest Guide

Following is a harvest calendar and a guide to the wide range of items available directly from farmers in the greater Bay Area.

Harvest Calendar of the Most Popular Items

Almonds—September, October
Apples—July—October
Apricots—June
Berries—June, July
Cherries—May
Corn—July—August
Figs—September—November
Kiwis—November, December
Melons—June—October
Nectarines—April—September
Oranges—December, January, February
Peaches—July, August
Pears—July—October
Persimmons—November
Plums—July, August
Prunes—August
Pumpkins—October
Tomatoes—August—October
Vegetables—June—October
Walnuts—October—December

Note: These dates are approximate. Always phone to make certain the desired produce is available.

What Is Available (Partial List)

Almonds, apples, apricots, artichokes, asparagus, beans, berries, broccoli, cabbage, carrots, cherries, Christmas trees, corn, cucumbers, eggplants, eggs, figs, flowers, garlic, gourds, grapefruit, grapes, green beans, herbs, honey, Indian corn, kiwi, lavender, leeks, lettuce, lemons, mandarins, melons, nectarines, okra, olives, onions, oranges, peaches, pears, peas, pecans, persimmons, peppers, pistachios, plants, plums, potatoes, prunes, pumpkins, red currants, rice, squash, sugar cane, tangelos, tomatillos, tomatoes, vinegar, walnuts, water chestnuts, and yarrow.

June Outings

The Beaches of Santa Cruz and Capitola

When Bay Area schools recess for the summer vacation in June it often seems half the families in the Bay Area load their children into the car and head for Santa Cruz. The reason is not difficult to discover. Santa Cruz beach is one of the most pleasant beaches in the Bay Area. It is large and sunny with little or no wind and it has gentle waves. A short walk up Santa Cruz beach is the interesting Municipal Pier. But best of all, located right on the beach is the Boardwalk.

The Boardwalk

The Boardwalk is a large amusement park with a variety of rides and games. One of the most popular rides is the Giant Dipper—a one-half mile long, thrilling roller coaster that dips up and down on a giant wood frame. The Giant Dipper is considered one of the best roller coasters ever built. The most charming ride is probably the merry-go-round. The merry-go-round has hand-carved wood horses dating from 1911.

However, if you can deny yourself the pleasures of the Boardwalk, the other beaches in Santa Cruz and nearby Capitola are less crowded.

Natural Bridges State Beach. The beach at Natural Bridges State Park is excellent for both swimming and surf-fishing. There are also many tidal-pools to explore. The best feature of the Natural Bridges State Beach is the beautiful landscaping which gives it a park-like setting.

Twin Lakes State Beach. Twin Lakes State Beach has a long sandy beach that is popular with local residents. It has fire pits. Within walking distance there is a small boat harbor and a lagoon with many ducks.

Capitola City Beach. Capitola City Beach is located in Capitola which is a small town with many arts and crafts shops. Nearby there is a wharf and a stream to explore.

New Brighton State Beach. New Brighton State Beach is popular with campers. In addition to swimming and fishing there are picnic sites and hiking trails.

Sea Cliff State Beach. Sea Cliff State Beach has a very long beach. In addition to swimming and fishing it has picnic areas and a 400-foot long concrete ship which is used as a pier.

Consult the Ready Reference—Celebrations & Outings for details

July

Grasshoppers

July Gardening

In Bloom

Annuals: impatiens, lobelia, marigold, petunia, and zinnia
Perennials: agapanthus, felicia, geranium, and Shasta daisy
Bulb-like: dahlia, gladiolus, tuberous begonia, and lily
Shrub: hibiscus, gardenia, and oleander
Vines: bougainvillea, clematis, and star jasmine
Crape myrtle

Fertilize everything in bloom or in the budding stage, particularly fuchsias, tuberous begonias, and roses. If the soil is dry, water well before fertilizing.

Throughout the summer pick off faded flowers when you see them. If flowers are allowed to remain they set seed which cuts back flower production.

Shear back overgrown, straggly, brownish growth on lobelia, felicia, petunia, and sweet alyssum. This produces new growth and flowers.

Watering Potted Plants

When you forget to water potted plants during warm weather, the soil may shrink away from the pot's edge. When watering is resumed, the water fails to penetrate the dried root ball and instead cascades over the hard soil surface and out the bottom of the pot without wetting the interior roots.

There are two solutions. The first is to submerge the pot in water, weigh it down, and not remove the pot until all the bubbling stops. The second is to buy a soil penetrant at a garden supply store (also called a wetting agent). When added to water the penetrant makes water wetter and more likely to penetrate the dried soil.

Watering the Garden

Gardens are lush in July if well watered. Passing over the garden with a hand-held hose does not count. Plants need a good, deep soaking to produce strong, drought-resistant roots.

In addition to watering, mulching is another way to maintain moisture in the soil. Apply two to three inches of oak leaves or pine needles for acid-loving plants such as azaleas, camellias, hydrangeas, and rhododendrons. Other plants can be mulched by leaves, compost, manure, ground bark, and gravel or rocks.

In the Nursery Look for:

Annuals: ageratum, chrysanthemum, marigold, and petunia
Perennials: agapanthus, felicia, geranium, and marguerite
Container grown: daylily and tuberous begonia
Shrubs: gardenia and hibiscus
Crape myrtle

July may be a warm and comfortable month for Bay Area gardeners but it also may be a little overwhelming for tender transplants. Set out new plants in the late afternoon or evening and provide temporary shade for two or three days.

Nurseries are well stocked with flowering annuals in July. Expect months of continual bloom from annuals such as ageratum, chrysanthemum, marigold, and petunia.

Tip-pinch chrysanthemums to make them bushy.

Bearded iris are both handsome and easy to grow. Nurseries carry iris rhizomes in July. This is the first of three months (July, August, and September) to plant or divide bearded iris. See August gardening for more information.

Pick up and dispose of fallen fruit and vegetables to avoid spreading fungus spores (such as brown rot) and to thwart the invasion of pests such as worms, slugs, and white flies.

Prune berry vines when you have finished harvesting the fruit. Ever-bearers may still yield more berries.

Vegetable Gardens

There is still time to plant a second crop in the vegetable garden. Plant bush beans, carrots, and radishes.

Hold off planting winter vegetable transplants since the really hot weather occurs in September and October.

Sow seed of winter vegetables, however, and transplant them in the vegetable garden when summer vegetables finish producing.

Gardenia and Hibiscus

The wonderfully fragrant gardenia and the exotically beautiful hibiscus are in nurseries this month. Both need lots of summer heat to bloom. In the cooler sections of the Bay Area plant gardenia and hibiscus against a white wall for reflected heat.

July Gardening Extra

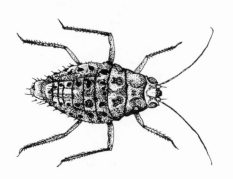 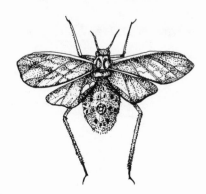

Aphids

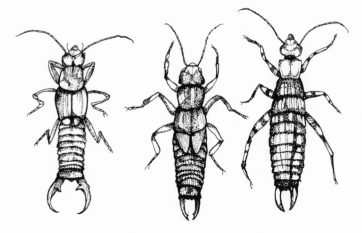

Earwigs

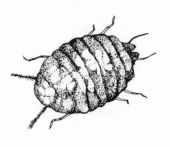 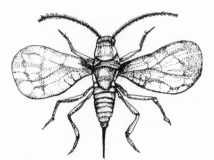

Scales

Grasshoppers

Garden Insect Pests and Their Removal

Most garden insect pests commonly found in Bay Area gardens can be chemically destroyed. Unfortunately insect predators are killed as well as the insects. There are several gardening practices that help reduce the insect pest problem.

① Spray garden plants with water—particularly soapy water. This reduces the aphid population. It also washes off dust that encourages mites and scale.

② Clean up debris. Debris is the preferred breeding ground of many insects, particularly earwigs.

③ Encourage birds that eat garden pests.

④ Hand pick slugs and snails. Some people stomp them, others collect them in a can and pour salt over them. Slugs and snails are voracious eaters and must be stalked persistently.

⑤ Consider systemic insecticides. These insecticides work through the plant to kill only insects that attack the plant.

⑥ Set out rolled newspapers at night to trap earwigs. The next morning collect and dispose of the newspapers in a covered garbage bin.

July Foods

Corn

The fresher the corn the better. Purists bring the water to a boil on the stove and then run into the garden to pick the corn. There is ample reason for this concern—hour by hour the sugar content of corn converts to a starch, which diminishes the corn's sweetness. When buying corn look for small, plump, evenly-spaced, soft-yellow kernels. Large, bright-yellow kernels are over-ripe and will be starchy and tough. Pale, white, watery kernels will lack flavor. Cook corn the day you buy it—cook it briefly, overcooking makes corn tough.

Eggplant

Eggplant is abundant in July. It is often used only in a few dishes: *ratatouille*, eggplant Parmesan, and *moussaka*. Too bad. Eggplant is a versatile vegetable; it is easier to use in other ways.

Eggplant is well suited to the barbecue season. Grill it over hot coals, then chop it with onions, garlic, and mayonnaise. Or skewer eggplant with tomatoes, onions, and bellpeppers to roast over the coals. Look for the small, elongated Japanese eggplant which is widely available in the Bay Area.

Tomatoes

Tomatoes are available year round but they only have that mature, sun-ripened, field-grown flavor for a few summer months. Look for tomatoes with a deep, rich, red color; they have been left on the vine the longest. Try the sweeter, pear-shaped Italian tomatoes; these meaty tomatoes are great in salads as well as sauces. Peel a tomato easily by dunking it in boiling water for one minute or by spearing it on a fork and holding it over a gas flame.

Zucchini Blossoms

Zucchini blossoms have a wonderful flavor. They are delicious when trimmed of their stalks, coated in a batter (preferably made with beer), and then deep-fried. They are also good sauteed and added to scrambled eggs or to an omelet. Zucchini blossoms can sometimes be purchased from Italian produce markets.

When picking zucchini blossoms from your own garden do not pick the female blossoms which have a tiny zucchini forming just below the flower. Pick the male blossoms which grow from thin, wiry stems.

Peaches

Peaches are grown in the San Joaquin Valley near Modesto. They are at their best in July and August. They must sweeten on the tree. Avoid peaches with an immature, greenish cast; it is a sure sign that they have been picked too young.

Contrary to the popular conception, the nice, rosy blush on a peach is not an indication of its character. Instead look for a background color of yellow or cream. Your nose will tell you which ones are ready to eat. A ripe peach has a wonderful, fragrant scent.

Most people think peaches taste better slightly chilled. Skin peaches easily by dropping them into boiling water for one minute and then plunging them into cold water.

Melons

The melon season begins in earnest in July. All melons must mature on the vine; if they are picked too early they will never get sweeter. As a judge of maturity, look for stem ends with sunken, well-calloused scars. Melons will, however, ripen off the vine, and the flavor will mellow becoming richer. That is why it is important not to refrigerate melons when you buy them; let them ripen a few days. Chill them four to five hours before serving.

Cantaloupes come to market from nearby Los Banos. Mature cantaloupes have thick, coarse webbing in bold relief over a yellow-orange, not green, skin. An easy dessert is produced by filling wedges of cantaloupe with Cointreau liqueur and then chilling them for a few hours.

Casaba melons are just coming onto the market in July. This melon is sweet and juicy when mature. A mature casaba melon should have a golden-yellow skin and a slightly soft blossom end.

Crenshaw melons are also just coming onto the market in July. This delicate, superbly flavored melon should be a deep, golden yellow.

Honeydew melons are mature when they have a creamy white color (not green) with patches of raised netting on a velvety skin.

Persian melons are mature when they have a thick, bold webbing (not a dark webbing) and a slight yield at the blossom end.

Watermelons can be conveniently judged by looking at the underside which should be yellowish not greenish. Watermelon should be served truly cold. To spike a watermelon, make two holes topside, pour in white wine and let it soak. Chill at least two hours.

July Celebrations

Fourth of July (Independence Day)—July 4

With fireworks, parades and speeches we celebrate the adoption by the Continental Congress of the Declaration of Independence which broke our colonial ties with England—a federal and legal holiday.

San Francisco has free family fun at Crissy Field in the Presidio, west of the St. Francis Yacht Harbor. From 3 to 8:30 P.M. there are folk singers, military bands, food vendors, and a children's show. Beginning at 8:30 there are spectacular fireworks over the bay.

Redwood City has a parade and fireworks.

Berkeley has fireworks at the Berkeley Marina.

Oakland has fireworks at Lake Merritt.

Half Moon Bay has fireworks at the beach.

Marin County has fireworks at the fairgrounds.

The Great American Arts Festival—San Jose

The festival is a multi-cultural extravaganza—musicians perform jazz, rock, western and big band music, plus there is folk dancing, and 300 booths of arts, crafts, and ethnic food on the Fourth of July weekend.

San Francisco Fair—San Francisco

The San Francisco Fair is a grand urban version of a county fair with hundreds of displays and performances, plus a parade, carnival and competitions. The location and month vary from year to year.

Tanabata (Star Festival)—San Francisco

One of the oldest and most romantic Japanese festivals, the Star Festival celebrates the yearly reunion of the heavenly lovers—the Princess Weaver Star (Vega) and the cowherder star (Altair.) The festival is usually held on the weekend closest to July 7, with colorful decorations, traditional song, and dance at the Japan Center.

Carmel Bach Festival—Carmel

There are concertos and symphonies by Bach and his contemporaries, plus lectures, panel discussions, and recitals at the Carmel festival. Candlelight performances are held in the basilica of Carmel Mission.

Marin County Fair—San Rafael

The Marin fair includes fine arts and crafts, floriculture, rides, a midway, and a national film festival at the Marin County Fairgrounds.

Bon Festival—San Francisco

The Bon Festival is also known as the Obon or the festival of the souls. It is a Buddhist celebration held mid-July in the Japan Center, and it is renowned for the Bon Odori, a community dance attracting hundreds of costumed dancers.

Obon Festival—San Jose

The San Jose Obon Festival, a Japanese-American cultural festival, is held the second weekend in July and includes games, dances, and food.

Gilroy Garlic Festival—Gilroy

Gilroy is the Garlic Capital of the World. The Gilroy festival's Gourmet Alley has open-air kitchens selling every imaginable food flavored with garlic. There are displays and demonstrations—over 100 booths with garlic braids, wreaths, and jewelry. The fair is held the last weekend of July or the first weekend of August.

Concours d' Elegance—Lafayette

Over 200 classic and vintage cars are on display at the Lafayette Concours d' Elegance—usually held the second Sunday in July.

Polk Art Fair—San Francisco

During the Polk Art Fair hundreds of arts and crafts booths line Polk Street from Sutter to Jackson.

Feast of Lanterns—Pacific Grove

The Feast of Lanterns is a large community celebration featuring a fashion show, a pet parade, entertainment at the pier, a barbecue, a pageant, and some fireworks.

The California Rodeo—Salinas

The California Rodeo is the largest rodeo in California; in fact it is one of the Big Four of the rodeo circuit right up there with the Cheyenne Frontier Days, the Calgary Stampede, and the Pendleton Round-up. It is a two-ring western extravaganza with classic cowboy events in one ring and another event on the horse-race track.

Remember the day, even the month, of an event may change. Consult the Ready Reference—Celebrations & Outings for details.

July Outings

Russian River

The Russian River is located north of San Francisco, between Highways 1 and 101. It is a popular destination for Bay Area residents in July. The river is a beautiful blue-green color; it has both rocky and sandy beaches and a dense-green shoreline growth which generally hides much of civilization. Best of all, the river wanders through towering redwoods and firs. The unfortunate news is it is usually crowded.

Country Roads

A look at a map of the area will show there are many access routes to the Russian River area such as the Gravenstein Highway, the Guerneville Road, and the River Road. All are back country roads. One of the joys of this area is to meander among them.

Resort Towns

Guerneville is the area's biggest town. During the summer it experiences a drastic population explosion. Other resort towns are Cazadero, Monte Rio, and Duncan Mills.

Cazadero Highway branches off Highway 116 and follows Austin Creek six miles to Cazadero. Cazadero receives more winter rain than any place else in Sonoma County. In the summer it is a quiet logging town. Duncan Mills is located at a point which is about as far as the ocean tide will reach into the Russian River. It is a favored spot with fishermen. Jenner is a fishing village located where the river meets the Pacific Ocean. It is a mecca for driftwood collectors.

Canoes for Hire

Many beach resorts rent canoes. Paddling down the river is one of the most popular activities on the Russian River. Reservations are recommended. The rental fee includes use of the canoe, paddles, and life jackets plus canoe transportation and a ride back to your car. Canoe trips can last several hours to several days.

Beaches

The most popular and crowded beach is Johnson's Beach in Guerneville. (Music concerts are sometimes held at Johnson Beach.) Another well-known beach is the beach in Monte Rio located near the bridge. Watch the road for signs indicating smaller beaches.

Armstrong Redwood State Reserve

Armstrong Redwood State Reserve is located two miles north of Guerneville. The 752-acre, virgin redwood park was donated as a preserve by a mill operator before the turn of the century. There are many large redwoods—the tallest one is over 300 feet. (One redwood felled near Austin Creek was said to be 23 feet in diameter.) There are easy trails to large redwood groves. During July and August, the Forest Amphitheater (accommodating 2,000 people) is frequently the site of free concerts on Sundays.

Fort Ross

Twelve miles north of Jenner on Highway 1 is Fort Ross State Historic Park. The fort was built in 1812 by Russian fur seal and otter hunters. The fine, soft dense fur of the California sea otter was highly valued by the imperial courts of Russia. The 14-foot tall stockade the Russians built was armed with 40 French cannons, spoils of war after Napoleon's defeat. By 1841 the sea otter was virtually exterminated and the Russian colony was having trouble with grizzly bears and crop failures. They evacuated, selling a lot of their goods to Swiss immigrant John A. Sutter. Visitors can view the restored wood chapel, stockade, and commandant's house. There is an entrance fee.

Occidental

Occidental is something of a phenomenon—a small town tucked into the redwoods that seems to support itself by feeding people, lots of them, out of several hearty Italian restaurants.

The reasonably priced meals are variations on a common theme such as antipasto, salad, minestrone soup, ravioli, an entree of chicken, duck, or steak with side dishes of chicken livers and zucchini pancakes. The meal concludes with a dessert such as apple fritters.

Three of the restaurants are the Union Hotel, Fiori, and Negri. All are worthy of a visit; each has a slightly different appeal.

Union Hotel is the oldest (1876), "funkiest", and most casual.

Fiori is the fanciest, quietest, and offers the widest selection.

Negri is comfortable, charming, but also noisy.

Details on a trip to the Russian River are given in the Ready Reference—Celebrations & Outings.

July Outings

The Sacramento Delta

Compared with Yosemite or Emerald Bay, it would seem inaccurate to call the flat, grey-green landscape of the Sacramento Delta beautiful.

Yet the Delta bog land bordering Highway 160 between Antioch and Sacramento is unique and haunting. There is the rich peat smell, and the feel of hot wind lifting off the Delta waterways. There is the glare of flat lands stretched out beyond a levee road, here a tract of water, there a pear orchard or a field of corn.

Small Adventures

Visiting the Delta is like going to another country if you are accustomed to landmarks of mountains and hills. The flat land is disorienting and it is easy to become lost. Venturing off the main road you may find the road ends abruptly amid the squawking geese of someone's farm. Or you may turn a corner and suddenly find yourself at a ferryboat crossing where, sure enough, a small, free ferryboat is coming to take you to the other side.

Certain places require a boat to visit such as the enchanted, hyacinth jungle of The Meadows or the ramshackle, funky Lost Isle. But car travel allows you to see what the high levees cut off from view of the boat travellers.

The Delta is a place to meander through—the experience is the trip not the destination. Highway 160 from Antioch to Sacramento is the scenic main route.

Places to Visit

Brannan Island has a state recreation area with sloughside picnic and swimming areas. A fee is charged to enter.

Rio Vista is located across the bridge over the Sacramento River; it is an interesting small town with a museum—the California Railway Museum located on Highway 12.

Isleton is a small town with a picturesque old dredger, the Neptune.

Ryde, located at a bend in the road, has the prohibition era Ryde Hotel with a speakeasy in its basement.

Locke is a clapboard, balconied, well-weathered Chinese settlement with boardwalks, and the *Dai Loy* Chinese Museum.

Courtland has the Bank of Courtland, an elegant reminder of the Delta's heyday. Courtland holds a pear festival in late July.

Staying

Overnight accommodations in the Delta country are limited. There are a few small, bend-in-the-road places with cabins to rent, and campgrounds for tents and recreation vehicles. There are also the already mentioned Ryde Hotel and Brannan Island State Recreation Area which has 100 campsites—reserve through Ticketron.

Eating

There are a few, small eating places along Highway 160—most of them are clapboard buildings which seem to promise roadside adventures. There are also restaurants such as the Riverview Lodge Restaurant in Antioch (on the San Joaquin River), the Point Restaurant in Rio Vista (riverside view), and farther up there is the dining room in the Ryde Hotel, and Moore's Riverboat on Andrus Island, plus at Locke, Al's Place—famous for steaks and peanut butter sandwiches.

Boating

It is possible to rent small power boats from local marinas, but be sure to call ahead on busy weekends. Houseboats that sleep 4-10 people are available from a number of operators. Obtain brochures and rates by writing the sources listed in the Ready Reference—Celebrations and Outings (Delta). Rates are cheaper mid-week and off season.

Two-hour cruises are available from Stockton. Day-long cruises from San Francisco to Sacramento (two days round trip) are available from Sacramento or San Francisco. Four-day long stateroom cruises can be booked through a travel agent.

Ferryboats

It is possible to take a short but free ferry boat ride. A convenient loop is made by taking the road outside of Rio Vista that runs north alongside the Sacramento River (not Highway 160 which runs along the other side of the river) to the Ryer Island Ferry. On Ryer Island follow Ryer Road East to Howard Landing Ferry, crossing to Grand Island. Once on Grand Island a right turn will bring you shortly to the road to Ryde and back onto Highway 160.

For more information on an outing to the Delta consult the Ready Reference— Celebrations & Outings under Delta.

July Outings

Tilden Regional Park

Tilden Regional Park is located in the hills above Berkeley. This 2,000-acre park seems removed from city life. It feels like wilderness with a few, magical places built by fun-spirited dwarfs.

The Nature Area

The Nature Area is one of the few places in Tilden where you can park your car and take in several activities. The Little Farm is a small farm with a wide variety of farm animals to visit and touch. Next door is the Environmental Education Center with museum-like displays and self-teaching exhibits. Nearby is Jewel Lake Boardwalk—an interesting boardwalk twisting through thick, marsh-like growth. At the end of the trail is Jewel Lake with a large population of ducks and turtles. All activities in the Nature Area are free.

Lake Anza

Lake Anza is located near the middle of the park. For a fee, visitors enter a beach area for swimming and sun-bathing. No fee is charged to hike, picnic, and admire the view. Visitors may also fish (those over 16 need both a State License and a Regional Park Permit). Swimming season is generally from May through September.

Other Areas

The Merry-go-round is a beautifully restored carousel set off on a knoll looking out to stands of pines. It is a dreamy experience. There is also a small shop attached selling fluffy, pink cotton candy.

The Little Train is another special activity set by itself at the far end of the park near South Gate entrance. A modest fee is charged to ride the model railway.

For the pleasure of children there are pony rides, again in a separate area near the middle of the park. For the pleasure of adults there is an 18-hole championship golf course, and for everyone—tennis courts and a field set aside for flying miniature airplanes.

There is also the Botanic Garden of native California plants which has streams, waterfalls, and steep paths.

Consult the Ready Reference—Celebrations & Outings for the telephone numbers of listed activities.

August

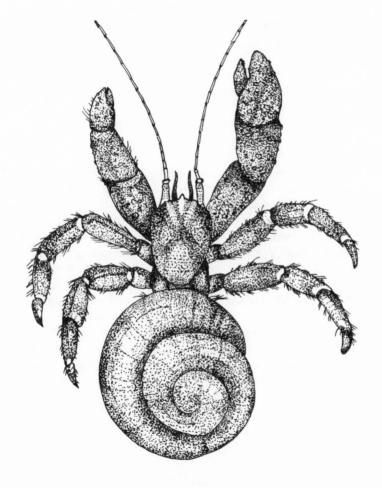

Hermit Crab

August Gardening

In Bloom

Annuals: ageratum, impatiens, marigold, sweet alyssum, and petunia
Perennials: aster, begonia, campanula, geranium, and phlox
Bulb-like: dahlia, tuberous begonia, and gladiolus
Shrubs: fuchsia, hydrangea, lavender, and rose
Vines: bougainvillea, clematis, jasmine, and passiflora
Crape myrtle

Fertilize azaleas, camellias, hydrangeas, and rhododendrons with acid fertilizer. Fertilize all plants now in bloom with an all-purpose fertilizer. Chrysanthemums should be fertilized until buds show color.

If your lavender is in bloom, see September gardening.

Sow seeds of winter blooming flowers such as sweet alyssum, calendula, pansies, and violas.

Harvesting Onions

When the green tops of your submerged onions stop growing, bend them gently toward the ground to hasten ripening. When the leaves have begun to wither dig up the onions. Lay them in the sun on a dry place for a week or two until the skins are papery. A raised chicken wire frame is perfect for air circulation. Do not let them get wet. It probably will not rain in August but protect the onions from dripping fog or morning dew.

Stringing Onions. Stringing onions is simple. Do not cut off the tops. Hang a three inch loop of string over a hook and pull it taut. Pick up the first onion by its long, dried top and put it through the middle of the loop then over one string and around the back all the way to the front and then down through the middle. Weave additional onions on top—alternate adding them from the right to left. Hang the onions in a cool dry place.

Harvesting Garlic

When the garlic leaves are dry, carefully fork up the garlic and dry them as for onions.

Braiding Garlics. Garlics are usually braided rather than strung. Braiding garlic is the same as braiding hair or braiding rope. As you braid add another garlic whenever you braid an outer stem into the center. Hang the braided garlics in a cool dry place to store.

In the Nursery Look for:

South African bulbs: clivia, freesia, ixia, watsonia
Lilium candidum bulbs (Madonna lily)
Bearded iris
Winter vegetable transplants

Sow onion seeds or plant onion sets in a sunny spot. Unlike most plants, onions like firm soil, so press down around the seeds or sets.

Set out winter-garden vegetables during the next months. When space is available plant broccoli, Brussels sprouts (remember they grow quite tall), cabbage, cauliflower, leeks, and lettuce.

Clivia Miniata

Clivia miniata, also known as kaffir lily, is a perennial grown from tuberous roots. It does quite well in the Bay Area. *Clivia miniata* has handsome, sword-shaped leaves and brilliant orange flowers that bloom from late winter to early spring.

Lilium Candidum

Lilium candidum, also known as Madonna lily, is a fragrant, white, June-blooming lily. During August it is dormant—prime time for planting. Plant it in a sunny location.

Bearded Iris

Bearded irises grow one to four feet tall depending upon the variety. Plant them in a sunny place. Water deeply two to three times during the summer. Fertilize lightly just before or after bloom. That is all the fuss this good-natured plant requires in return for magnificent flowers that rival orchids for exotic beauty.

Dividing Iris. After four years iris have reproduced so many off-spring that they bloom better if divided. Fork up the iris clump carefully and pull the plants apart. Cut away the old woody center, leaving a healthy, little thumb attached to the fan of leaves. To make handling easier cut off all but eight inches of the leaves and roots. Let the cut dry several hours or overnight. Plant the divided iris shallowly, about six inches deep, fanning out the roots. The plant expands outward from the fan of green leaves so point the fan in the direction you want growth to take. Water well after planting.

August Foods

Figs

Sadly, many Americans outside of California have never eaten a fig. California's Mediterranean climate lends itself to fig growing. California's best-known fig is the black-skinned Mission fig which should be purchased really black and dusky looking, even on the withered side, for true sweetness. Also look for the yellow–green-skinned Calimyrna and Kodota figs.

Nectarines

Nectarines reach their peak supply in August. There are many varieties but all of them should have a slight softness along the seam to assure a fully ripe, sweet fruit.

Pears

August begins the pear season. First to appear is the sweet, popular Bartlett which is usually yellow, tinged with pink but it can also be all red (a variety known as the 'Max-Red Bartlett'). Later this month you may encounter the smaller, quite sweet, brown-yellow 'Seckel' which has a grainy texture.

In October the winter pears appear. Yellow-green 'Anjou' looks like a rounder 'Bartlett'—it has a sweet, somewhat winy flavor. Russet-colored 'Bosc' is tart and crisp textured. 'Comice' is large with superb texture and flavor.

Pears are picked and sold hard—you have to ripen them yourself at home. Let them sit in a warm place until the stem end is soft to the touch, usually about three to five days. To cook with pears use them while still firm.

Tomatillos

Tomatillos are the small round fruit of the *Physalis ixocarpa* bush. They are picked green and used in Mexican cookery. They have a unique, exotic taste that most people find agreeable. When canned, they are usually labeled Mexican green tomatoes although tomatillos are not related to tomato plants.

To cook fresh tomatillos, remove the papery calyx and boil them until soft. Drain and mash them. They are usually combined with chili, garlic, fresh coriander, and onions to make a sauce. They are available fresh from Mexican markets and some produce stores.

Bay Area Cheeses

What could be easier for August picnics than a selection of tasty cheeses and a fresh baked baguette? Bay Area cheese makers produce some unusual and delicious cheeses. Inquire at a local cheese shop periodically about locally made cheeses—they appear sporadically and are new even to cheese books. The following is a brief guide to two types of cheese made in the Bay Area, Jack cheese and goat cheese, and to crème fraîche which is often carried by cheese shops and is splendid on top of August's fresh figs and raspberries.

Sonoma Jacks

Two cheese makers in Sonoma, the Sonoma Cheese Factory and the Vella Cheese Company, make delicious Jack cheeses. Look for their high moisture, handmade wheels of cheese—the open hole texture results in a softer, more flavorful Jack. These cheeses are often combined with caraway seeds, onions, hot green peppers, or garlic. Also look for the nuttier Dry Jack—it is perfect with red wine and, because of its better keeping qualities, it is also perfect for backpacking.

Chèvres

One of the most interesting of the new cheese makers is Laura Chenel, proprietor of her own *fromagerie* in Santa Rosa. After studying production techniques in France, she began making her own goat milk cheeses. Examples of her cheeses are Pyramides (ash covered or plain), Castile (with or without herbs), Goat Fourmé (with a more pronounced goat flavor), Cabeçon (wrapped in a grape leaf or marinated in olive oil and peppercorns), or the fresh Fromage Black de Chèvre.

Crème Fraîche

Crème fraîche is not a cheese but it is listed here because many cheese shops that carry locally made cheese also carry locally made *crème fraîche*. *Crème fraîche* is a French-style cream high in butterfat —sour cream is 18% butterfat compared to *crème fraîche's* 30% butterfat. This thick, somewhat nutty (not sour) cream can be boiled without curdling. It is used on fresh fruit, in desserts, and in cooking.

The Ready Reference—Foods lists cheese shops likely to carry local cheeses and crème fraîche.

August Celebrations

Concord Jazz Festival—Concord

During the Concord Jazz Festival major jazz artists perform over a three-day span in the Concord open-air pavilion.

August Moon Concerts—St. Helena

During the August Moon Concerts, classical music is performed out-doors at the Charles Krug Winery. There is wine tasting at intermissions.

Pacific States Crafts Fair—San Francisco

Top west coast craftspeople exhibit and sell their work at the Pacific States Crafts Fair. There are also demonstrations and seminars.

Peddler's Fair—Benicia

The Peddler's Fair is known for its antiques and soon-to-be antiques— it is usually held the second Saturday in August.

Castro Street Fair—San Francisco

Hundreds of arts and crafts booths line Castro Street in San Francisco's elegant gay area on the third Sunday in August. This is one of the first street fairs to incorporate stage shows.

Cupertino Art and Wine Festival—Cupertino

The Cupertino festival includes crafts booths, entertainment and food. It is usually held the first weekend in August.

Victorian Days—San Mateo

A fashion show, with entertainment and food, is sponsored by the San Mateo County Historical Society, usually on the last weekend in August.

Art and Wine Festival—Hayward

The festival includes art, wine, and food at the B Street Plaza.

Los Gatos Cultural Festival—Los Gatos

The festival includes continuous entertainment, a barbecue, and an arts and crafts sale—usually on the fourth weekend in August.

Renaissance Pleasure Faire—Novato

The Renaissance Pleasure Faire recreates an outdoor harvest festival of Elizabethan England with music, dance, foods, games and pageantry.

Napa Town and Country Fair—Napa

The Napa fair includes livestock exhibitions and auctions, flower exhibits, music, entertainment, viticulture exhibits and a wine garden, a kiddie carnival, and ethnic cooking.

Santa Clara County Fair—San Jose

The Santa Clara fair features a variety of exhibits and nationally known music stars—usually in the second week of August.

Campbell Highland Games—Campbell

Competitions include Scottish dancing, piping, caber toss, traditional Scottish foods, clan tents, and bag pipe bands.

Mill Valley Film Festival—Mill Valley

The Mill Valley Film Festival is a celebration of film and video, with screenings, and a screen writing and playwriting workshop. There is a gala opening night party usually the first weekend in August.

Concours d' Elegance—Pebble Beach

The Pebble Beach event is one of the grandest car shows with hundreds of cars including vintage Rolls Royces, Packards, and Bentleys.

Old Adobe Fiesta—Petaluma

The fiesta, at the Adobe State Historical Park, features music, dancing, and the homely arts of pioneer days.

California State Fair—Sacramento

The state fair is held in the California Exposition complex (built in 1979) which is designed with a series of waterways to enhance the fair-going experience. Each year the fair has a different theme with special events. There are always events such as livestock shows, horse shows (past years have included a Cavalcade of Horses—an introduction to the different horse breeds), a vast agriculture display of products, viniculture exhibits and wine judging, a carnival, and in recent years 14 acres of water world which contains the world's largest water slide. The fair usually runs August into September.

Remember the day, even the month, of an event can change. Consult the Ready Reference—Celebrations & Outings.

August Outings

Stinson Beach and Duxbury Reef

August, the last of our calender summer months, is traditionally a month to go to the beach. One of the most popular beaches for Bay Area residents is Stinson Beach. The projecting mass of Point Reyes Peninsula often protects Stinson Beach from the great fog bank that invades many Northern California beaches. The approach to Stinson Beach along Highway 1 as it skirts Mt. Tamalpais through groves of eucalyptus trees is one of the most pleasant drives in the Bay Area.

Stinson Beach State Park

Stinson Beach is a state park with a long, gently sloping beach front. It is an excellent family beach with lavatories and an outdoor shower. Picnic tables and grills are set among the trees bordering the beach and parking lot. There is also a snack bar. The parking lot is large and there is almost always a parking space available. A fee is charged to enter the parking lot.

One of the interesting features of Stinson Beach is the sand spit which stretches three miles beyond the town of Stinson Beach toward Bolinas—it is usually possible to find a place all to yourself along the sand spit. The swimming is good at Stinson Beach but chilly like most Northern California ocean beaches. There are lifeguards in the summer. Another enjoyable feature of Stinson Beach is the view back toward the hills which is almost as pretty as the ocean view.

The small village of Stinson Beach is a quiet, pleasant place oriented toward residents as much as toward tourists. Nearby Bolinas is a town noted for crafts shops and summer bungalows built over the water on pilings. Duxbury Reef located just beyond Bolinas is an excellent place to observe a variety of marine life. Tidal pool life typical of Northern California is illustrated on pages 113 and 114. Duxbury Reef, which has many tide pools, is discussed on page 115.

Consult the Ready Reference—Celebrations & Outings for details on an outing to Stinson Beach.

The **hermit crab** is pictured on the August cover. It is a crustacean that hides a portion of its body in someone else's shell—usually a turban snail shell. As it grows it moves to a bigger shell; major crab wars are fought over housing rights.

Sea Anemones

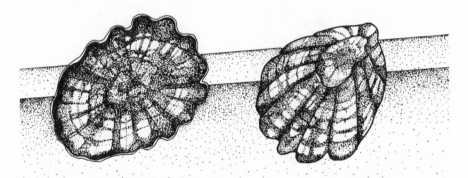

Limpets

Sea anemones are flowerlike animals. They fold inward when threatened or when feeding. They are carnivorous—their tentacles can inject a paralyzing compound into their prey. Some can reproduce by dividing in half or by growing a whole new anemone from a severed piece.

Limpets are one-shelled mollusks. They creep over the rocks in high tide, scraping off algae with rasping radulae (tongues). They return to the same protected spot such as a crevice. Limpets can live up to fifteen years.

August Outings

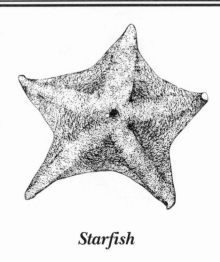

Starfish

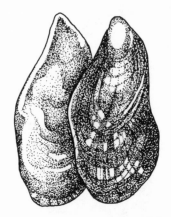

Mussels

The **starfish** is a marine animal, not a fish. It can pry open a shell with its arms—usually it has five arms—and then evert its lower stomach into its victim's shell to digest the victim. It can also regenerate severed arms. Certain species of star can regenerate a whole new starfish from a severed arm.

Mussels are two-shelled mollusks. They open their shells to eat, drawing the water through with their cilia (hair-like structures). In Europe and England, they are a popular food but in August they are an unwise choice in the Bay Area. From May through October mussels from Northern California beaches can be poisonous.

Duxbury Reef

Duxbury Reef is a huge shale reef extending a mile into the Pacific Ocean from Bolinas Point near Agate Beach (a county park). The reef is a reserve managed by the California Department of Fish and Game. At a minus tide it is possible to walk one-half mile or so out on the reef examining the tidal pools. Daily newspapers carry tide tables—consult the newspaper to time a visit to coincide with a minus or low tide.

Bolinas Lagoon

Duxbury Reef is not the only nearby area with sea life. The mudflats of Bolinas Lagoon are some of the richest, most intact salt water marshes on the Pacific Coast. The marsh life supports a large population of sea birds which are protected by several nearby preserves such as the Audubon Canyon Ranch (see May outings) and the Point Reyes Bird Observatory.

Tidal Pools

Ocean water rises and falls about every 12 hours and 26 minutes due to the gravitational pull of the sun and the moon. When the tide falls, tidal pools are exposed in the rocky tidelands.

Tidal Pool Precautions

★ Watch the water! Do not let the incoming tide cut off your safe return to shore. Also watch out for the waves.

★ Very important: do not disturb the tidal pools or the marine life will die!

★ If you pick up a rock to look under it, put it back exactly as you found it.

★ Do not pry loose attached animals.

★ Do not take animals home.

★ Please explain to others the importance of protecting intertidal plants and animals.

Other Northern California Tidal Pools

There are other excellent places in addition to Duxbury Reef to explore tidal zone life in Northern California such as Tomales Bay, Point Reyes, Moss Beach, Santa Cruz, Monterey, Pacific Grove, and the Fitzgerald Marine Reserve in Half Moon Bay.

August Outings

Lake Tahoe

Lake Tahoe is located a little over 200 miles east of the Bay Area. The remarkably blue lake is so clear that it is possible to see a white dinner plate 120 feet below the water's surface. It is also the largest Alpine lake on the North American continent—12 miles wide, 22 miles long, with a 72 mile shoreline.

August is a good month to visit Lake Tahoe—the weather is usually warm and dry although the nights can be chilly. The following are some of the many attractions of the Lake Tahoe area.

Donner Memorial State Park

The Donner Party was trapped in 22-foot high snow in the winter of 1846. Ultimately they resorted to cannibalism—their ordeal still haunts and fascinates. The Donner Memorial State Park has a museum which contains both Donner Party and Indian relics.

Squaw Valley

Squaw Valley was the site of the 1960 winter olympics. During the summer the Squaw Valley Tram carries visitors 2000 feet up to where it is possible to view both the peaks of the Sierra Nevada and the brilliant blue of Lake Tahoe. A hiking trail leads to Shirley Lake where swimming is available.

River Rafting and Inner Tubing

Several outfits in the Lake Tahoe area offer rafting trips on nearby rivers in both California and Nevada. Another popular river trip is the 4-mile float from Tahoe City to River Ranch on inner tubes.

Emerald Bay

Probably the most scenic attraction at Lake Tahoe is Emerald Bay. It is known for deep emerald-green water and silver-gray granite cliffs. The high road around Emerald Bay offers spectacular views.

D. L. Bliss State Park is a 1,237-acre forest park near Emerald Bay that offers a sandy beach and beautiful views of aquamarine Rubicon Bay. It also offers camping, hiking, swimming, and fishing.

Vikingsholm is a re-created ninth century Norse fortress also located at Emerald Bay. Tours of the 38 room castle-fortress are free. It is reached either by a steep one-mile hike from Emerald Bay or by boat.

Desolation Wilderness

Desolation Wilderness is a true wilderness of polished granite slopes, lonely meadows, and more than 70 lakes. It is the joy of backpackers and isolation seekers. June to October are good months to visit because the snows will cut off access by November—the snows will also stay on the ground in chilling patches until late spring or early summer. The 63,000-acre wilderness is under the supervision of the United States Forest Service.

Stateline

Stateline is located on the Nevada side of Lake Tahoe. Although it is compact in area it has a city "big time" atmosphere. It is famous for gambling and night life. There are four large casinos and two smaller gaming establishments. A full selection of Nevada-style gambling games are available 24 hours, seven days a week at Stateline.

Lake Tahoe Cruises

In summer there are a variety of boat cruises available on Lake Tahoe. The boats, some resembling old, paddle-wheel show boats, leave from a variety of places such as Lakeside Marina, Ski Run Marina, Zephyr Cove, and South Shore Marina.

Virginia City

Virginia City is located in Nevada less than an hour's drive from Lake Tahoe. In 1870 Virginia City had a population of 30,000 residents and 4 banks, 5 theaters, 6 churches, and 110 saloons. Today much of Virginia City has been restored to resemble its rowdy 1870 boomtown heyday. In fact it bills itself as "the liveliest ghost town in the West."

Shakespeare at Sand Harbor

During August an event known as Shakespeare at Sand Harbor is held in an outdoor amphitheater bordering the lake. Playgoers usually bring a picnic and blankets. These professional performances can be elaborate—for example the theater has staged fireworks over the lake during performances of *The Taming of the Shrew.*

See the Ready Reference—Celebrations & Outings for details on the many possibilities of a Lake Tahoe outing.

August Outings

Golden Gate Park

When the city of San Francisco purchased 1,000 acres of shifting sand dunes to create a park, the idea was greeted with ridicule. But the park that John McLaren created became one of the most renowned metropolitan parks in the world. Even more remarkable, it is a true people park—there is always something agreeable to do.

Sports

Feeling athletic? The park offers jogging, skating, tennis, handball, baseball, bicycling, and golf. At **Stow Lake** it is possible to rent row boats, pedal boats, and motor boats.

Horticulture

Feel in need of the solace only Mother Nature can offer? Then wander through the **Fern Dell**, the **Rhododendron Dell**, the **Fern Forest**, or visit **Strybing Arboretum**—60 acres with 3,000 varieties of trees and shrubs. Or treat yourself to the **Conservatory of Flowers**—the warm, humid, lush world of orchids and ferns.

Music and Art

Desire an enriching aesthetic? At 2 P.M. on Sundays and holidays, weather permitting, there is usually something playing at the **Music Concourse**. The **M.H. de Young Museum** and the **Asian Art Museum** offer significant collections from all over the world and many time periods. The two art museums charge an entrance fee.

Science Museums

Care to expand your knowledge? **The California Academy of Sciences** offers natural history and science exhibits—everyone seems to love the life-like dioramas of wild animals. Then move on to the **Steinhart Aquarium**—two areas bound to please are the Swamp which has alligators in a vivid setting, and the Fish Roundabout where visitors stand in the middle of a large aquarium and large ocean fish careen around them at dizzying speeds. Finally the **Morrison Planetarium** offers shows about the universe. There is an entrance fee to the museums.

Consult the Ready Reference—Celebrations & Outings for details of a visit to Golden Gate Park.

The Indian Summer Season

Temperature—warm to hot
mid fifties to high seventies

Indian summer is the season fog-shrouded residents long for—it is the Bay Area's true summer. How unfortunate that school is back in session; summer's strongest enthusiasts are corraled from enjoying it fully. It occurs precisely because the rest of California is adhering to typical calendar seasons. The Central Valley cools off with the waning of the summer sun and simultaneously that weight of cold air called the Pacific High moves south. The blanket of fog is no longer drawn across the Bay Area and suddenly relatively fog free, we are also free of its cooling influence.

Smog

But there is a catch to our Indian summer season. Without the cleansing winds created by the pushing of the Pacific High and pulling of the hot Central Valley we experience the metropolitan phenomenon called smog. Sometimes the smog becomes so dense it sets the fog horns bellowing.

Harvest Time

The grapes ripen in Napa Valley's vineyards making for a memorable excursion during the grape crush when the heady aroma floats on the warm valley air. In the foothills of the high Sierra apple growers offer fresh-pressed cider as well as apples by the bushel for sale. In the coastal haze of Half Moon Bay thousands of pumpkins are hauled down from the foothills and set in fields bordering Highway 1. Home gardeners harvest herbs and cooks make them into teas, sauces, and vinegars.

This is the best beach weather of the year, inspiring outings to Point Reyes where oysters can be purchased for beach side barbecuing. It is also fine weather to cross a fog-free bay for a picnic on Angel Island. The Bay Area's warmest season inspires many outdoor community activities over the Labor Day weekend plus several fall and harvest festivals.

A rain storm may blot the season but it is just as likely that Bay Area residents will have two months or more to enjoy the harvest season in comparative warmth.

September

Wine Country Picnic

September Gardening

In Bloom

Annuals: impatiens, lobelia, marigold, and petunia
Perennials: begonia, campanula, and Shasta daisy
Shrubs: fuschsia, hydrangea, lavender, and rose
Bulb-like: dahlia, gladiolus, and Japanese anemone

September is the best month for planting cool season lawns: bent, bluegrass, fescue, and rye. Cool season lawns begin a green growth spurt this month. Fertilize and water them well.

Fertilize begonias, fuchsias, and roses. Also fertilize all newly planted annuals, vegetables, and perennials after they are established for two weeks. Citrus plants get their final feeding this month.

Prune back overgrown, scrawny pelargoniums. Start new plants by rooting tip-cuttings that show no blooms.

Carefully dig up and divide overgrown agapanthus, daylily, primrose, and Shasta daisy.

Dig up and divide overgrown bearded iris—see August gardening.

September is prime time for planting landscape plants—trees, shrubs, and ground covers—so they can develop sturdy root systems over the winter and burst into top growth next spring.

Harvesting Herbs

As the rainy season and cold weather approach it is time to finish harvesting and drying herbs. Harvesting is also a way of pruning to produce bushier plants next spring. Clip herbs in the morning after the dew has dried.

Tie the herbs loosely in small bunches and hang them by the stems so the volatile oils flow into the leaves. Hang them in a dark, dry place with good air circulation. The exception is parsley which needs really high heat to dry properly. Dry parsley in the oven set at 150 °F with the door open. Herbs dry at varying rates; basil and sage take longer than most herbs. When a herb is truly dry strip the leaves by holding the tip of a stem in one hand and drawing the fingers of the other hand down the stem. The exception is mint to be used for tea—hand pick the leaves because you will want to use them whole.

Place the dried leaves in tightly sealed, labeled jars. Crush the dried herbs between your fingers when they are used in cooking. Some herbs may be used fresh in herb butters (which can be frozen) and in herb vinegars. See the September foods section.

In the Nursery Look for:

Annuals: calendula, chrysanthemum, Iceland poppy, and pansy
Perennials: felicia, pelargonium, and marguerite
Spring blooming bulbs, corms, tubers, and rhizomes
Container-grown shrubs and trees

Native California Plants

Fall is the best time to plant California native plants. Not only does fall planting take advantage of winter and spring rain, but water is applied in the seasons native plants are accustomed to being wet rather than in the hot, dry summer. Of course, new plants need to be watered until the rains come. They will also need to be watered the first summer or two, but after they are established, they require little attention from the gardener. Native plant societies hold plant sales in fall; many nurseries also carry native plants.

Spice Bush (*Calycanthus occidentalis*) is a little-known deciduous shrub that grows 4 to 12 feet high. Usually wider than it is high, it has shiny oval leaves and wonderful dark red-brown flowers that resemble miniature water lilies. Both the leaves and the flowers are aromatic. In fall the leaves turn light yellow before dropping. Native near streams and on moist slopes, it accepts ordinary garden cultivation.

Bush anemone (*Carpenteria californica*) is more widely known (and grown) in England than in California. This evergreen shrub grows 4 to 6 feet tall and has a rather formal, cultivated appearance as if it belonged in a park setting. Scented white flowers, resembling anemone blooms, appear in late spring or early summer.

Western redbud (*Cercis occidentalis*) is a large shrub or small tree (10 to 15 feet) that is attractive all year. In spring it is covered with magenta blossoms. In summer its rounded blue-green leaves dangle from the delicate limbs and dance with the breeze. In autumn the leaves turn red and yellow, then drop, revealing winter's silver-gray branches.

Flannel bush (*Fremontodendron*) a large shrub or small tree (8 to 12 feet), is stunning in spring when it is smothered with large, vivid yellow blooms. The cultivars 'California Glory,' 'San Gabriel,' and 'Pacific Sunset' have longer bloom periods than the species *Fremontodendron californicum.* Because the foliage scratches, plant it well back from walkways.

Matilija poppy (*Romneya Coulteri*) produces spectacular crinkly white flowers as large as dinner plates. This invasive perennial grows 6 to 8 feet high and should be planted in full sun at the back of a border away from less vigorous plants.

September Foods

Elephant Garlic

Elephant garlic is named after its huge cloves. It is not nearly as strong as the smaller, white-skinned American or red-skinned Mexican garlic. One interesting way to use elephant garlic is to smear it with oil and then bake it whole until soft. Then mash it into a paste to spread on bread. Elephant garlic is carried by some gourmet markets. It is also available from local garlic farms—see the Ready Reference—Foods under garlic.

Grapes

California grows most of the table grapes eaten in the United States. The most popular grape, the 'Thompson seedless,' is marketed from early summer to winter. When buying Thompson seedless grapes, look for a yellowish color with an amber cast for a sweet, fully ripe flavor. On the market in September are the red-skinned grapes such as the hard, crisp 'Malaga, Red' grape and the elongated 'Emperor.' Look for the purplish-red Tokay also called the Flame Tokay—it is grown locally near Lodi, and it is considered the best of the red grapes. Also on the market in September are the spicy muscadine grapes such as the yellow-skinned, sweet 'Muscat.' Refrigerate grapes and serve them chilled but not ice-cold. Wash grapes at the last minute before serving.

Barbecued Pacific Oysters

The large Pacific oyster (*Crassostrea gigas*) flourishes in the Bay Area. It is perfect for barbecuing in the backyard on warm September days. Buy oysters fresh from several companies in Tomales and Drake's Bay (see the Ready Reference—Foods), or from a local fish market.

To barbecue Pacific oysters it is best to have a hot fire. Mesquite wood charcoal (available in some supermarkets and many cooking supply shops) burns very hot. Heat the charcoal until the flame licks at the grill. Scrub the oysters with a brush to remove the grit and sand. Place the oysters on the grill with the deeper, cup side down. Carefully remove the oysters when their shells pop open slightly. They will cook in 3 to 4 minutes over a truly hot fire, and in 8 to 10 minutes over a less intense heat. You may have to finish opening them with an oyster knife—watch out; they are quite hot. Throw away the top shell. Serve them with melted sweet butter and lemon wedges, or with a garlic and parsley compound butter (see p. 126).

Northern California Wines

Gone are the days when Northern California wineries could be easily enumerated. Napa Valley alone has over 110, and Sonoma Valley has almost as many. Add to this approximate 200 Napa and Sonoma wineries, those of the Sierra foothills, those of Lake and Mendocino counties, and the coastal wineries centered around Santa Cruz—the number within easy driving distance of the Bay Area is mind-boggling. Additionally, every winery, of course, produces a variety of wines. Trying to comprehend all the Northern California wine labels is an attempt at permanent vertigo.

Wine Shops

A wine drinker's best friend in maneuvering through the pleasures available in local wine is the local wine merchant. Wine shops exist throughout the Bay Area—their primary business is knowledge of wine.

Wine Classes

If you decide to become your own wine expert, you will find plenty of encouragement in the Bay Area. Classes in wine appreciation are offered by universities, adult education schools, wine shops, cooking schools, and wine societies. Casual tastings are offered on selected wines (usually changed twice a week) by wine shops and bars. Organized tastings are also offered—at these serious tastings, wines are discussed and compared. They usually include food and require prior enrollment.

Local Bay Area Wineries

You do not need to drive to Napa or Sonoma to visit a winery. Locally, within city limits, there are wineries with tasting rooms.

The Takara Sake USA Factory in Berkeley has a tasting room for their varieties of Japanese rice wine.

In the Pleasanton and Livermore area there are Concannon Vineyard, Wente Brothers, and Stony Ridge Winery.

In the San Jose area there are Paul Masson Champagne and Wine Cellars, Mirassou, and Weibel Champagne.

In San Anselmo there is Grand Pacific.

Addresses and telephone numbers for these wineries are listed in the Ready Reference—Foods, under wineries.

September Foods Extra

Using and Preserving Herbs

Bouquet garni is the herb bouquet used to flavor sauces, soups, stews, stocks, and braised meats. A fresh bouquet is made of 4 sprigs of parsley, 2 sprigs of thyme, and ½ bay leaf bound together with twine. A dried bouquet is made of the above dry, crumbled ingredients tied into a cheese cloth bag.

Herb salt is easily made. It is used as a general seasoning.

1½ cups chopped fresh herbs (such as oregano or marjoram with chervil or parsley, plus thyme)

1 cup non-iodized salt

Blend the salt and the herbs in a mortar for 5 minutes. Preheat the oven to 250 °F then turn it off. Spread the salt mixture on a cookie sheet and place it in the oven until dry.

Herb vinegar can be made by many different recipes. This one is potent because it is reduced by boiling. It can be tamed later by diluting the finished vinegar with more vinegar.

1 cup fresh herbs (chervil, dill, tarragon, or basil)

1 pint boiling cider or wine vinegar

1 clove garlic, peeled

Place the herbs in a large, non-metal container and crush them slightly with a wooden spoon. Pour the hot vinegar over the herbs and add 1 clove of garlic. When the vinegar is cool remove the garlic and cover. Let the vinegar steep two weeks. Then strain the vinegar through several layers of cheese cloth into a large sauce pan. Discard the herbs. Boil the vinegar rapidly, uncovered, for 15 minutes. Pour the finished vinegar into sterilized bottles and cork tightly.

Herb compound butter can be stored in the refrigerator for a few days or it can be frozen.

1 pound of fresh sweet butter

2 tablespoons lemon juice

6 tablespoons minced herbs (use basil, or marjoram, or tarragon, or use oregano, parsley, and 2 cloves of garlic together.)

Cream the ingredients together in a blender or food processor. Pack the butter into decorative crocks or shape it into a cylinder to be tightly wrapped, frozen, and sliced as needed.

Mint

There is no such thing as growing a little mint—once established, mint advances rapidly on the rest of the garden. The following are two recipes for utilizing bountiful mint.

Mint jelly is easy to make when making apple jelly. Simply add a bushy branch of mint to each of the canning jars and pour in the hot apple jelly. Swish the branch around while adding a few drops of green food coloring. The wonderful aroma will tell you that within minutes the mint is dominating the apple. Remove the mint and cover the jars.

Mint tea (also called a tisane or an infusion) is also easy to make. Warm a china tea pot by adding hot water and then dumping it. Use 4 to 6 fresh mint leaves per cup (or 5 to 7 dried mint leaves). Place the leaves in a bamboo strainer or cheesecloth inside the tea pot. Pour water brought to a rolling boil over the leaves and let it steep 3 to 5 minutes. Remove the mint, and serve with honey or sugar.

Basil

Use the last of the season's basil in a salad dressing to be used within a week, and in a pesto which can be frozen to be used later.

Pesto is used fresh or frozen in dollops wrapped in plastic wrap.
3 cups basil leaves (or part parsley)
3 cloves peeled garlic
6 walnut halves
¾ cup olive oil
A twist or two of freshly ground black pepper
½ cup freshly grated Parmesan or Sardo cheese
Blend everything but the cheese in a mortar with a pestle, or in a food processor, or a blender until it is a thick paste. Then add the cheese, blending only a few seconds to mix it in.

Basil and mint salad dressing is a refreshing combination. To make the dressing add 2 tablespoons minced fresh basil, and 2 teaspoons each minced mint and chives to ⅔ cup salad oil and let the flavors marry for 3 hours. Then add ⅓ cup rice vinegar ½ teaspoon salt, ¼ teaspoon ground pepper and blend well.

September Celebrations

Vacaville Onion Festival—Vacaville

Food and entertainment help celebrate the onion harvest.

A La Carte, A La Park—San Francisco

This is a a feast for gourmands on Labor Day weekend when restaurants pitch tents and musicians perform in Sharon Field in Golden Gate Park.

Concord Fall Fest—Concord

On Labor Day weekend, this festival includes grape-stomping, live music, crafts, and food booths in Santos Park in Concord.

Pan Pacific Exposition Art and Wine Festival—San Francisco

This celebration of the 1915 World's Fair at Marina Green features ragtime music, food, and penny-farthing bicycle races.

Pacific Coast Fog Fest—Pacifica

A celebration of the mascot mist with arts and crafts, parade, seafood, oyster-shucking, music, and family fun.

Millbrae Arts and Wine Festival—Millbrae

On the two days of Labor Day weekend, the Millbrae festival includes handmade arts and crafts, wine tasting, keepsake glasses and mugs.

San Anselmo Country Fair Day—San Anselmo

Fair day includes townwide sales, arts and crafts, games and music.

San Jose Harvest Festival—San Jose

Over 500 costumed craftspeople re-create a 19th Century American county fair as they entertain and sell their wares and food.

Sausalito Art Festival—Sausalito

The festival has arts, crafts, sculpture, entertainment, and food.

Handicraft Fair—Benicia

The fair features a variety of handcrafted arts and crafts plus food.

Autumnal Equinox—September 22 or 23

The autumnal equinox marks the onset of autumn on the day the sun crosses the equator and day and night are of equal length.

Scottish Gatherings and Games—Santa Rosa

The Santa Rosa event is a celebration of the Scottish culture with traditional Scottish games, Highland dancing, and bagpipe bands.

Fall Festival (Aki Matsuri)—San Francisco

The three day Fall Festival, held at the Japan Center, features a variety of traditional Japanese events such as Taiko drumming, a tea ceremony, kendo, and cooking demonstrations.

Aki Matsuri—San Jose

The San Jose Aki Matsuri is held outdoors and features classical Japanese dancing, Taiko drumming, singing, brush painting, and food.

Fall Festival—Castro Valley

The two day Fall Festival is held on a weekend in downtown Castro Valley. It features wine tasting, arts and crafts, and food booths.

Almaden Valley Festival—San Jose

The Almaden Valley Festival features arts and crafts, entertainment, and wine tasting on the third Sunday in September.

Russian River Jazz Festival—Guerneville

The Russian River Jazz Festival has open-air concerts performed at Johnson's Beach. Bring a picnic and a blanket.

Monterey Jazz Festival—Monterey

The Monterey Jazz Festival is an internationally renowned series of jazz concerts performed by major and upcoming jazz artists.

San Francisco Blues Festival—San Francisco

The San Francisco Blues Festival consists of a variety of blues-style music performed in the Great Meadow at Fort Mason.

National Begonia Festival—Capitola

The festival includes a sand sculpture display, a crafts fair, and a parade of flower-decorated boats that float along Soquel Creek.

Remember the day, even the month, of an event may change. Consult the Ready Reference—Celebrations & Outings.

September Outings

Point Reyes Peninsula

The blunt headlands and grass-tufted dunes of Point Reyes Peninsula are located 50 miles north of the Bay Area. Projecting far out into the Pacific Ocean, the peninsula is lopped-off on one side by Tomales Bay and intruded on the other side by Bolinas Lagoon. September is an excellent month to visit the peninsula—the protected beaches on the Tomales Bay side can reach a water temperature of over 80 degrees.

Oysters

During the drive to the peninsula you can see the commercial oyster beds of Tomales Bay. They are fenced in with redwood stakes to keep out the sharks. The large Pacific oyster is grown both in Tomales Bay and Drake's Bay. To grow the oysters, fertilized oyster eggs are spread on strings of oyster shells and then suspended in water. They are hauled out for harvest.

There are several places to buy oysters for beach-side barbecues. Jensen's Oyster Beds and the Tomales Bay Oyster Company both are located near the boat works town of Marshall. Johnson's Oyster Company is located across the bay past Inverness on Sir Francis Drake Boulevard.

Telephone numbers are given in the Ready Reference—Foods under oysters. It is best to check the hours of operation before you drive out. Directions for barbecuing oysters are given in the September cooking section. Point Reyes beaches with barbecues include Heart's Desire Beach (which is part of Tomales Bay State Park) and Drake's Beach (which is part of Point Reyes National Seashore at Drake's Bay).

Point Reyes National Seashore

With or without oysters, stop at the park headquarters, which is located one-fourth mile west of Olema, to obtain a map and current information on beaches, trails, and exhibits.

Near the park headquarters is an authentic reproduction of a Miwok village. Once there were more than 100 Miwok villages on the peninsula. To walk among the Miwok dwellings is to appreciate a way of life that flourished at the time of Drake's visit. Also near park headquarters is an earthquake trail which points out the continental drift and indicates the results of fault movement. The peninsula shifts northward about two centimeters per year.

Bear Valley

Bear Valley is a paradise for hikers and solitude-lovers. Located behind park headquarters is the trailhead leading to nearly 100 miles of trails. Carry a canteen since the trail water is nonpotable.

Limantour Spit

Limantour Spit is a slender finger of sand dunes two miles long. It ends across the water from the white cliffs of Drake's Bay. The area is suitable for sunbathing, wading, and bird-watching. To reach the spit take Bear Valley Road from park headquarters approximately two miles to Limant-our Road which ends eight miles later at Limantour Spit.

Drake's Beach

Drake's Beach is a pleasant, broad, swimming beach with the beautiful white cliffs some historians think were those that reminded Sir Francis Drake of the white cliffs at Dover. A long drive through Inverness down Sir Francis Drake Boulevard leads to Drake's Beach.

Tomales Bay State Park

Tomales Bay State Park is located a mile or two past Inverness on Sir Francis Drake Boulevard. An entrance fee is charged. The picturesque cove called Heart's Desire Beach is a warm, calm, swimming area and a fine wading area for children. A one-half mile trail through a forest leads to a similar beach called Indian Beach.

McClure's Beach

In contrast with calm bay beaches, McClure's beach on the ocean is fierce with thundering surf (no swimming) breaking on large rocks. Pierce Point Road leads across the northern peninsula to McClure's Beach. The actual beach is reached by a one-half mile, steep access trail. There are tide pools at low tide.

Point Reyes Beach

Point Reyes Beach is twelve miles of white sand beaches and grass-tufted sand dunes. It is a beach for walking, not swimming.

For further information see the Ready Reference—Celebrations & Outings (Point Reyes Peninsula).

September Outings

Napa Valley

Late September is grape harvest time in Napa Valley—which is located forty-five miles north of the Bay Area. During September the picked grapes are piled high in open gondolas and the heady aroma of crushed grapes permeates the valley. A visit to Napa Valley during harvest time is a memorable outing.

Plan to visit only two or three wineries a day, taking plenty of time to enjoy the experience much as you would savor a good wine. All the wineries listed here are well-established wineries offering tours. The smaller, newer wineries are often too occupied with the grape harvest to offer tours at this time. The wineries are listed in the order in which you would encounter them once past the town of Napa driving north on Highway 29.

Christian Brothers—Mont Lasalle is located to the west on Redwood Road amidst acres of rolling vineyards. The stone winery dates from 1903. This winery is also a novitiate, which is a religious training ground for future Christian Brothers. Try their Chateau LaSalle which is made from sweet muscat grapes.

Domaine Chandon is located to the west, just before Yountville. It is housed in an award-winning building and owned by France's largest champagne producer, Moet-Hennessy. In addition to their acclaimed sparkling wines, there is a beautiful and expensive French restaurant.

Vintage 1870 is located to the east, as you pass through Yountville. It is a complex of galleries, antique and specialty shops housed in an imposing brick building that was formerly a winery.

Oakville Grocery is located in Oakville. The grocery is the parent store of the elegant gourmet San Francisco market of the same name. It is renowned for outstanding produce, some of it locally grown, plus bread, cheese, and wine.

Robert Mondavi is located to the west, passing through Oakville. This modern winery has a reputation for innovation. Their tour is considered to be one of the best.

Inglenook is located to the west as you enter Rutherford. The ivy-covered Inglenook winery has a romantic appearance complete with cupolas. It was founded in 1879 by a Finnish sea captain.

Beaulieu is located in Rutherford. The ivy-covered winery was founded in 1900 by a Frenchman named George de Latour.

Louis Martini is located to the east, beyond Zinfandel Lane. The plain-looking winery has a reputation for good value. Their tour is considered particularly instructive.

St. Helena is the small compact main town of the wine area. It dates from 1853. North of town notice the high vault of elm trees.

Beringer is located to the west, just after Spring Mountain Road. It was founded in 1876 by two German brothers whose impressive Rhine House serves as the winery visitor's center.

Christian Brothers is located to the west, beyond Beringer. It is the second Christian Brothers' tasting and touring location. This one is called Greystone. It was founded in 1888. There is a large corkscrew collection on display.

Charles Krug is located to the east, just past the road to Christian Brothers. This reliable old stone winery was founded in 1861. During the summer a concert series uses the old coach house as a background.

Old Baly Mill is a landmark located about four miles north of St. Helena. The grist mill was built in the 1840s.

Boethe-Napa Valley State Park is located about a mile beyond the mill. This large, wooded park offers camping, creek fishing, hiking, and a swimming pool.

Hanns Kornell is located to the east on Larkmead Lane. This smaller winery produces fine sparkling wines using traditional methods.

Sterling is located to the west. The winery is a striking white structure perched on a hill. To tour, take the aerial tramway (fee applied to wine purchase) to the winery. The tour is self-guided.

Calistoga is the usual turn-around point for Napa Valley visits. The town is famous for its hot springs and glider rides. (See March outings—Calistoga.)

The Ready Reference—Celebrations & Outings (Napa Valley) gives more details on a visit to Napa Valley.

September Outings

Angel Island

Located in the San Francisco Bay and accessible only by boat, Angel Island is neither a wilderness nor a cultivated park land. It is a place where humans have conquered and then vanished—the roads are still there but not the cars. It is a fine place to idle away a sunny September afternoon by walking and imagining the island's past.

Down by the bay, for example, squaring up to the San Francisco waterfront, is a vacated garrison. It is a hundred years old and its window eyes are glassless. Its board skin is a beautiful splintered gray. It stirs the imagination more than if it had been all gussied up. There are other relics hunkered down on the island's flat lands.

Ferry Boats

Most visitors arrive on ferry boats from San Francisco or Tiburon. See the Ready Reference—Celebrations and Outings under Angel Island for more information on the ferries. There are also mooring and docking spaces for private boats at Ayala Cove.

Picnicking

The park service charges a small entrance fee when visitors step off the boat onto the island. Picnicking is most convenient on the grassy knoll at Ayala Cove near park headquarters. There are barbecues, restrooms, and a snack bar.

Hiking and Walking

The walk around the island on the paved road takes a little over two hours. There are several hiking trails up Mount Caroline E. Livermore. Some of the trails are quite steep. The 360 degree view from the peak makes the hike worthwhile. There is a helicopter pad at the top—a reminder of the island's past as a missile site.

Elephant Train Tour

During the peak summer months, usually including part of September, there are one-hour-long narrated open coach tours. Tour guides narrate the island's varied past and the history of the remaining buildings.

For details consult the Ready Reference—Celebrations & Outings under Angel Island.

October

Pumpkins

October Gardening

In Bloom

Annuals: impatiens, marigold, lobelia, and petunia
Perennials: Japanese anemone, begonia, and chrysanthemum
Sasanqua camellia
Shrubs: hydrangea and rose

Dig up and divide overgrown perennials such as agapanthus, daylily, primrose, and Shasta daisy.

Clean up garden debris to deprive insects, snails, and slugs of their winter haven.

Fertilize azaleas, camellias, and rhododrendrons with 0 - 10 - 10 fertilizer. This no-nitrogen formula encourages bud formation.

Lawns

October is the last month to start a new lawn. Fertilize bent, bluegrass, fescue, and rye lawns. Water your lawn well and mow it with a lawn mower blade set at 1½ inches. Reseed bald spots.

Native Plants

This is the best month for planting native California plants, which is why native plant societies hold sales this month. Native plants are featured on pages 35, 122, and 165. Be sure to plant them in a well-drained site. If rains have not arrived yet, water native plants now.

Roses

October is a good month to review your rose garden. Roses that bloom sparsely or have much mildew might do better if transplanted later this winter to a sunnier location. While roses are still in bloom, visit a local rose garden and decide which bare-root roses you might want to purchase this winter.

Fertilize roses for the last time before October 15th. Remove faded blossoms. Always cut back to a five leaf stem to encourage new bloom.

Winter Gardens

October is a good month to plant a winter garden. Cool season crops include vegetables such as bok choy, broccoli, Brussels sprouts, cabbage, carrot, cauliflower, chard, Chinese cabbage, garlic, leek, lettuce, onion, radish, and spinach.

In the Nursery Look for:

Trees and shrubs from containers
Sasanqua camellias in bloom
Spring blooming bulbs, corms, tubers, and rhizomes
Winter bedding plants

October is an excellent month for planting landscaping plants such as container grown trees and shrubs.

Sasanqua camellias thrive in the Bay Area. They bloom heavily in fall and early winter. They are also more tolerant of sun than the more commonly known *Camellia japonica.* Nurseries sell them now.

Winter Blooming Plants

Calendulas have large orange or yellow flowers. Plant these annuals in the sun. They are subject to mildew.

Cinerarias are perennials in areas influenced by marine weather. They have bright colored, daisy-like flowers. Plant them in the shade.

Primroses have cheery, brightly colored flowers. These hardy perennials prefer shade and lots of water.

Iceland poppies have amazing, fragile flowers atop willowy stems. Plant these annuals in full sun.

Pansies and **violas** are perennials with small but cheerful looking flowers. Plant them in part sun. Often they will self-sow.

Spring Bulbs

Shop for spring blooming bulbs, corms, tubers, and rhizomes such as, anemone, crocus, daffodil, Dutch hyacinth, Dutch iris, freesia, leucojum, narcissus, ranunculus, scilla, and tulip. Look for plump, top-quality bulbs. Chill tulip and hyacinth bulbs in the refrigerator for six weeks and wait until November to plant them.

To plant the bulbs first dig the soil to loosen. Add sand to clay soil. Work one tablespoon of steamed bone meal into the soil beneath each bulb. Plant large bulbs (daffodil size) six inches deep and six inches apart, with the pointed ends up. Plant small bulbs (crocus or freesia sizes) three inches deep and three inches apart, with the pointed ends up. Cover with soil and water well. For continuous bloom, plant anemones and ranunculus every three weeks until December. Sow sweet alyssum or California poppy seed for a thick, quick cover.

October Foods

Apples

The onset of fall weather begins the major apple season. Unfortunately many commercial apples have been hybridized for long shelf life and beauty rather than flavor. The following is a brief guide to what is commonly available in the Bay Area.

'**Red Delicious**' is America's best-selling apple. It is a big, red apple easily recognized by the five bumps at the blossom end. It is sweet and rather bland.

'**Golden Delicious**' is a large, pale-green apple. Like the 'Red Delicious,' it is sweet and rather bland. It is good for diced salads since it does not turn brown as quickly as other varieties.

'**Wine Sap**' is dark red apple with a distinctive tart flavor. It is good for eating raw and for cooking in pies and applesauce.

'**Rome Beauty**' is a dark red apple accented with yellow. It has a mildly tart flavor and superior baking qualities.

'**Newtown Pippin**' is a greenish yellow apple that is grown in nearby Watsonville and Sebastopol. It is a favorite of commercial pie companies because it is wonderfully juicy and tart.

Pears

The queen of the pears, 'Comice', is at its peak in October. Choose bruise-free pears and ripen them in an evenly warm spot two or three days until there is a slight give when pressed.

Dungeness Crab

The west coast crab season is approximately from October through May. The flavor of Dungeness crab changes throughout the season—the best tasting crab is caught early in the season. For the best flavor, also choose the largest crab (2½ to 3½ pounds) which serves two.

Late Harvest Wines

Autumn weather is perfect for savoring the complex, semi-sweet wines made from late harvest grapes. To purchase these unique wines visit a wine shop—not a liquor store—and ask for California wines made from late harvest grapes. Examples of late harvest wines are wines such as, Late Harvest Joseph Phelps Johannisberg Riesling, Late Harvest Fenestra Chenin Blanc, San Martin (Santa Clara) Johannisberg Riesling, and Monte Vina Mission del Sol.

Fresh Pumpkin Pie

To prepare a pie from a pumpkin first wash and cut the pumpkin in half from stem to stern. Remove the seeds and the strings. Set it on a cookie sheet, shell side up and bake it at 350 °F for one hour until it is tender and begins to fall apart. Scrape the pumpkin meat from the shell, and force it through a strainer or whirl it in a blender or a food processor until it is smooth.

Use the prepared pumpkin puree in any pumpkin pie recipe or use the following recipe.

2 eggs, slightly beaten	½ teaspoon ginger
2 cups cooked pumpkin	½ teaspoon nutmeg
(or canned pumpkin)	¼ teaspoon cloves
½ cup white sugar	1 teaspoon cinnamon
¼ cup brown sugar	1¾ cups (14 fl. oz.)
1 teaspoon salt	evaporated milk or cream

Preheat oven to 450 °F. Mix the above ingredients in the order given until they are well blended. Pour the mixture into an unbaked pie shell. Bake 15 minutes. Reduce temperature to 350 °F and bake 45 minutes longer until a knife inserted in the center comes out clean. Cool and serve with whipped cream.

Roasted Pumpkin Seeds

Pumpkin seeds are flavorful and nutritious. To bake them, first wash the seeds. Remove most of the pumpkin strings and pat the seeds dry with paper towels. Coat the inside of a bowl with butter or egg white then toss the seeds with ½ teaspoon of salt for each cup of seeds. Spread the seeds over a cookie sheet and roast them in a 250 °F oven, stirring frequently until brown (approximately 15 to 30 minutes.) Let them cool before eating.

Nasturtium Blossoms and Leaves

Nasturtium blossoms and leaves are edible. The bright orange color of the flowers is well-suited for October dining. The flowers can be floated on soups, or shredded to add color to tossed salads. The leaves have a peppery flavor—cut into small bits and add to hot potato salad or mixed vegetables.

October Celebrations

Native plant sales—Bay Area

Native plant societies hold plant sales in October, often on the first weekend—watch for this opportunity to buy rare and unusual plants.

Harvest Festival—Fremont

Celebrate the autumn season at historic Ardenwood Farm with cider-pressing and the harvesting of pumpkins, walnuts, and wheat. There are also demonstrations of farm machinery and square dancing. Experience life before the automobile with old-fashioned wagon rides.

Italian American Cultural Festival—San Jose

The week-long San Jose festival ends on the weekend closest to Columbus Day. It includes opera, tarantella dances, authentic Italian food, a Saturday night street dance, and a Sunday open-air mass.

Halloween—October 31

Halloween day is derived from the rites of Druids on Saman when the Lord of Death called together the souls of the wicked who had died during the year. It is celebrated with costumes and trick-or-treats.

Pumpkin Weigh-off and Pumpkin Fair—Half Moon Bay

The Half Moon Bay street fair includes arts and crafts, food booths, and special events—see October outings for more information.

Art Festival—Piedmont

The Art Festival includes art and entertainment in the Piedmont park.

Fleet Week—San Francisco

Fleet Week is scheduled for mid-October from Thursday through Sunday. During this time naval vessels are open to the public and the Blue Angels aviation team performs over San Francisco.

Arts and Crafts Fair—San Bruno

The San Bruno street fair includes arts, crafts, and food plus day-long entertainment on the first weekend in October.

Sunny Hills Grape Festival—San Rafael

The Sunny Hills Grape Festival includes arts and crafts, a grape booth, music, wine tasting, and sometimes a hot-air balloon show.

Octoberfest—Bay Area

German clubs in several Bay Area cities celebrate the German culture at harvest time with German dancing, foods, games, and special events.

Octoberfest—Lake Tahoe

The Lake Tahoe Octoberfest is held the fourth weekend in October with an old fashioned German Octoberfest—music, food, beer drinking, and dancing—and on Sunday afternoon a battle of the bands.

Tsu Kimi—Oakland

Oakland's Tsu Kimi is a tranquil moon viewing ceremony at the time of the full autumn moon. It is held at the Lakeside Park Center at Lake Merritt and includes traditional Japanese entertainment.

Apple Hill Growers Festival—Camino

The harvest is celebrated at apple ranches in the foothills of the Sierra Nevada with apple picking, cider, crafts, and entertainment.

Greek Festival—Hayward

The festival has Greek dancing, music, food, and cultural displays.

Sonoma County Harvest Fair—Santa Rosa

At the County Fairgrounds, there are exhibits of everything from grape-stomping to cooking with wine, plus wine displays and auctions.

Grand National Rodeo, Horse Show, and Livestock Exposition

The Grand National Rodeo is held at the Cow Palace in San Francisco. It includes top professional cowboys, fine horsemanship, and quality livestock. This is the last stop on the professional rodeo tour—every performance features a fine horse and western horse conformation show, plus rodeo and roping events. Try to arrive early enough before showtime to visit the barns and see the prize-winning livestock.

Butterfly Parade—Pacific Grove

The parade consists entirely of local school children. See November outings—Pacific Grove for information on the monarch butterflies.

Remember the day, even the month, of an event can change. Consult the Ready Reference—Celebrations & Outings for details.

October Outings

The Pumpkins of Half Moon Bay

Located twenty-five miles south of San Francisco, the coast with a name like a line of poetry once was a glimmer of commercialism in a railway developer's eye. But the "Coney Island of the West" never became a reality thanks to the rugged shoreline of Half Moon Bay, particularly the shoreline near the Devil's Slide area which made a rail line infeasible. During the Prohibition, the secluded beaches and coves of Half Moon Bay became the no-man's land of rum-runners and roadhouses.

Today, Half Moon Bay is a series of coastal communities and beaches stretching from Montara to Pescadero. It is a rural area of flower fields, shipyards, ranches, harbors, and farms. The area also caters to tourists, but quietly. Generally, these are the sort of towns you pass through on your way to somewhere else—but in October, Half Moon Bay becomes a destination.

Half Moon Bay Art and Pumpkin Festival

Half Moon Bay, the pumpkin capital of the West Coast, hosts a weekend Pumpkin Festival in October. The popular festival begins with a pumpkin weigh-off for pumpkins grown all over the United States. These pumpkins compete with Canadian pumpkins weighed in Nova Scotia.

The festival's activities are varied. They include an arts and crafts fair during the daylight hours over the weekend; a costumed children's parade on Saturday at noon, usually a haunted house, a pumpkin carving contest and a pie eating contest.

Pumpkins

Even without the festival, it is interesting to visit Half Moon Bay in October to see the pumpkins. They are brought down from the nearby hills and the Central Valley, and spread out over the fields along Highways 1 and 92 beginning in the first week of October.

Pilarcitos Cemetery

In keeping with Halloween's spirit, you may want to visit Pilarcitos Cemetery—located on Highway 92—a pioneer cemetery dating from 1820.

The Ready Reference—Celebrations & Outings lists details for an outing to Half Moon Bay.

Pumpkins and Scarecrows

During the last week of October, the Nut Tree Restaurant in Vacaville holds the Great Scarecrow Competition with close to three hundred versions of scarecrows. These whimsical, artistic creations are spread out in the fields behind the restaurant along with hundreds of pumpkins for sale.

The Nut Tree is set in a walnut grove with a small train shuttling the guests to the restaurant's private airstrip. Airplane memorabilia are featured in the large shopping pavilion which also features homemade candy and bread. The address and telephone number are listed in the Ready Reference—Celebrations and Outings under pumpkins.

Pumpkin Patches

It is possible to pluck your own special pumpkin off the withering vine. The harvest guides listed in the Ready Reference—Celebrations and Outings list the local pumpkin patches. For the convenience of readers a few of these pumpkin patches are also listed in the Ready Reference—Celebrations and Outings under pumpkins. When visiting a pumpkin patch, always phone first for business hours and directions.

October Outings

Apples, Old Sacramento and Nevada City

October is a good month to drive to the foothills of the Sierra Nevada in search of autumn color—the leafy reds and golds of oak and locust, and the willowy yellow of cottonwoods. It is a four to five hour drive to reach the apple country near Nevada City, but the monotonous freeway pace can be varied by taking Highway 4 to Highway 160 which meanders alongside the twisting Sacramento River.

The alternate route provides a glimpse of Delta life—high levee roads, croplands, orchards, and flat stretches of Delta waters. See July outings—Delta Country for more details. Once past Freeport look for the Interstate 5 signs to return to Interstate 80. To reach the Sierra foothills, go east on Interstate 80 toward Reno. You might, however, want to visit Old Sacramento for lunch or a rest break.

Old Sacramento

Old Sacramento is 10 blocks of a restored commercial district dating back to the gold rush era. It is a good place to dine or to stretch your legs along the boardwalks. The historic character of Old Sacramento is maintained in the museums, saloons, and shops. Old Sacramento is located between Interstate 5 and the Sacramento River on Embarcadero. There is no admission fee.

California State Railroad Museum

The California State Railroad Museum is located in Old Sacramento at Second and I streets. The museum documents the history of the railroad in the United States. There are over 20 locomotive engines and rail cars impressively displayed. An admission fee is charged.

Sutter's Fort

Sutter's Fort is another interesting stop in Sacramento. To reach Sutter's Fort exit Old Sacramento and take 3rd Street to N Street—past the state capitol—to 28th and L Streets where Sutter's Fort is located. Sutter's Fort was the first white man's fort in the interior of California. The restored adobe house was built in 1839. There are relics of both pioneer and gold rush days. Adjacent to the fort is the state Indian Museum which documents Indian culture in California through displays of baskets, clothing and art. To continue to Nevada City take 29th to Interstate 80.

Apples

At Colfax turn off Interstate 80 onto Highway 174 toward Grass Valley. This 15 mile stretch is apple country. Apple ranches along this route sell apple cider, apple pie, and crates of apples.

Nevada City

Nevada City is one of the best preserved gold mining towns in California. It was once the third largest city in California. Part of Nevada City's charm is that it is still a living city, not a monument. The past clearly dominates street after street of wood-framed, gingerbread houses, and stores with broad front porches and ornate balconies.

Once Nevada City was one of the most important cities in California. Lincoln came here to campaign in 1864 and so did Grant several years later. Nevada City is the county seat of Nevada County which yielded over one-half of the total gold production in California.

There are several outstanding places to stay such as, the Victorian Nevada City Hotel built in 1854; the very small, very ornate Red Castle, and the unique and isolated Kenton Mine Lodge and Cookhouse, which is located 45 miles north of Nevada City.

Old Nevada Theater

The refurbished Old Nevada Theater dates from 1865. It is thought to be the oldest theater building in California. The theater stages both plays and musicals.

Firehouse Museum

The Firehouse Museum, housed in a firehouse dating from 1861, displays a wide variety of pioneer and Indian artifacts.

American Victorian Museum

The American Victorian Museum is dedicated to preserving and exhibiting Victorian art and relics. The museum also houses a restaurant and a staging area called Old Stone Hall, which is used for cultural productions.

Details for planning an outing to Nevada City and Sacramento are in the Ready Reference—Celebrations & Outings.

October Outings

Carmel

October is probably the best month to visit Carmel. Not only is the summer tourist season over but there is less fog, more sunshine, and warmer temperatures than during any other month.

Carmel is a forest village of small shops offering crafts, clothing, and decorative items from all over the world. What Carmel village does best is offer America's favorite pastime—shopping—in an aesthetic setting guaranteed to be free of neon signs, towering buildings, garish advertisements, and even street numbers.

The quaint shops are covered with ivy and adorned with window boxes of blooming flowers. There are an abundance of odd little lanes and narrow passageways between buildings. The motels are called inns, and they compete for the tourist trade with garden settings, ocean views, balconies, and fireplaces. The restaurants are elegant or at least charming. Of course this appeals to a great many people and weekends are usually crowded, making reservations a necessity.

Carmel Beach

Carmel Beach is located at the end of Ocean Avenue, which is the main shopping street in Carmel. The beautiful beach has fine white sand, gnarled wind-swept cypress, and cresting turquoise waves. During October Carmel holds its annual sand castle contest.

Pt. Lobos Reserve Park

Pt. Lobos Reserve Park is located a few miles south of Carmel. The 1,200-acre state park was established to protect the California sea otter (see March outings) and to provide a breeding ground for the brown pelican (see November outings). The park has several interesting trails through the rugged seacoast terrain.

Carmel Mission

Mission San Carlos Borromeo del Rio Carmelo is a restored, early California mission built in 1797. Father Junipero Serra, a Spanish missionary who founded many California missions, is buried under the altar. There is also a museum that displays mission relics.

Consult the Ready Reference—Celebrations & Outings for details on a Carmel outing.

The Silver Season

The silver season is the forgotten season—expunged from memory by the excitement of the holidays. Neither hot nor cold, wet nor dry— it is also an ephemeral season caught between the gray rain clouds and the waning sunshine.

Rain

November often shares what is left over of the Indian summer. Sometimes as early as September, but certainly by November, the Bay Area will experience the first rain which makes the streets dangerously slippery. However the true wet season is still ahead and gardeners must remember to water their yards.

While the sun migrates south the daylight hours dwindle and the evening darkness arrives progressively earlier. Following in the wake of the sun, the Pacific High journeys south and once again storms sweep across the Pacific Ocean turning the silver season into a wet one.

Fall Migration

The sun is not alone in its migration south. November is an excellent month to observe the southern migration of birds and butterflies. Astride the Pacific Flyway, the Klamath Basin National Refuge attracts an estimated 10 million birds during the fall migration. In Pacific Grove, millions of orange and black monarch butterflies migrate from as far away as Alaska and the Canadian Rockies.

Holiday Foods and Performances

This is a season of feasting with three major holidays—Thanksgiving, Chanuka, and Christmas. Holiday food items such as chestnuts, cranberries and roasting game fowl come on the market place. Bakeries offer seasonal treats such as stollen and mincemeat pie. Zinfandel Nouveau is offered for sale—a young, recently bottled wine meant to be enjoyed without aging. This is definitely a season to be savored gastronomically.

It is also a season of holiday performances which are annual traditions such as *The Nutcracker* ballet, staged renditions of *A Christmas Carol*, and sing-a-long versions of Handel's *Messiah*.

Seasonal Reminders

In addition to the outings recommended for November and December, the following phenomena provide alternative seasonal excursions.

Pacific Gray Whales

Pacific gray whales migrate south along the Pacific coast. See January outings pages 10 to 11.

Elephant Seals

Elephant seals arrive at Año Nuevo in November and remain through March. See February outings pages 24 to 27.

November

Canada Goose

November Gardening

In Bloom

Annuals: calendula, sweet alyssum, and pansy
Perennials: begonia, chrysanthemum, and Japanese anemone
Sasanqua camellias
Autumn foliage and red-berried shrubs

Continue with fall clean-up. Pull up dying annuals and vegetables. Rake up leaves. Put away empty clay pots, nursery flats, and other garden items that could be used as winter havens for insects, snails, and slugs.

Stake chrysanthemums so they do not bend and break under heavy rain. When chrysanthemums finish blooming, cut them back 4 to 6 inches above ground level.

Water until ground-soaking rains come. Cooler weather and waning daylight hours make fewer demands on plants—water less heavily. But thoroughly soak newly planted annuals and winter vegetables.

There is still time to divide perennials such as, agapanthus, daylily, primrose, and Shasta daisy.

Autumn Foliage

Autumn is associated with leaves of yellow, red, and gold and with bright red ornamental berry plants. The following trees and shrubs bring fall color to a garden.

Acer (maple). Many maples do splendidly in cooler sections of the Bay Area. Japanese maple (*Acer palmatum*) is a small, delicate tree with vivid fall leaves. When the leaf edges of a Japanese maple turn a burnt brown, water heavily to leach out built-up salt in the soil.

Liquidambar (sweet gum). This large deciduous tree has a graceful form and wonderful fall color. The American sweet gum has an interesting prickly pointed fruit.

Nandina (heavenly bamboo). This delicate, airy shrub resembles a bamboo. Since it is small in scale—1 to 8 feet tall—it can be grown in a large pot as well as in the garden. Plant nandina in full sun for the best leaf color.

Cotoneaster. There are many varieties of this sprawling, red-berried shrub. Plant cotoneaster in full sun, away from a cultivated garden. It thrives on barren slopes. Many varieties of cotoneaster produce small white flowers in the springtime.

In the Nursery Look for:

Annuals: calendula, Iceland poppy, and pansy
Perennials: cineraria, cyclamen, primrose, and violet
Sansanqua camellia
Spring blooming bulbs, corms, tubers, and rhizomes

There is still time to put in a cool season lawn such as bent, bluegrass, fescue, or rye. Do not delay. Heavy rains could wash away carefully planted seeds.

November is a good month for setting out basic landscape plants such as trees, shrubs, and ground covers. Over the winter the roots will become well-established for spring growth.

Prepare the soil now—before it becomes too rain-soaked—for bare-root planting later.

Spring Bulbs

Tulips and hyacinths need at least six weeks in the refrigerator before planting. Other spring blooming bulbs can also be planted such as, anemone, crocus, daffodil, Dutch hyacinth, Dutch iris, freesia, leucojum, narcissus, ranunculus, and scilla. See October gardening for directions.

Wildflowers

November is a good month for sowing wildflower seeds. Nurseries, or the seed houses listed in the Ready Reference—Gardening, sell packets of mixed seeds. Part of the pleasure of sowing wildflower seeds is discovering what pops up next spring. Wildflower seeds have interesting names such as chinese houses, farewell-to-spring, mustang clover, tidy tips, and baby blue eyes.

Prepare for sowing, by clearing a space of weeds. Rake the area smooth to loosen the top soil. Wildflower seeds are usually tiny, so it is a good idea to mix them with sand so you can see where they land. Cast them evenly over the raked soil and then carefully rake them in or—better— scatter compost or soil amendment lightly over them. Be sure to cover the seeds to hide them from the birds.

Water, being careful not to wash away the seeds. Keep the soil moist until winter rains relieve you of the task.

Resume watering when the rains stop next spring. Wildflowers often bloom well into June.

November Foods

Cabbage

Once a cool-season crop, cabbages are now available year round. In addition to the common green and red cabbages there is the curly-leaf savoy cabbage and the crinkly-leaf Napa cabbage. Look for a firm head, heavy for its size. Refrigerate cabbage covered with plastic.

Chestnuts

Fresh chestnuts are a luxury for roasting in the fireplace or adding to the Thanksgiving stuffing. Remove both the outer shell and the bitter inner skin. The two most common methods involve making an x cut on the flat side of each shell. Then boil the chestnuts for 15 minutes covered and remove a few at a time to shell and skin. Or else dribble the x cut nuts with oil and roast 15 minutes at 400 degrees, then shell and skin. But the most romantic method is to build a fire in the fireplace and line the uncut, unoiled chestnuts near the hot coals. Roast, turning frequently, until you hear them pop. Be careful—the chestnuts will be very hot!

Fennel "Sweet Anise" or Finocchio

Fennel resembles a bulbous celery. It has a mild licorice flavor. The thick base is sliced thin in salads or braised as a vegetable. The leafy tops are used as an herb in compound butters, marinades, stuffings, soups, and sauces. The stalks are dried and used underneath an oily fish like tuna or mullet when barbecuing. Fennel has an affinity for fish and makes a good side dish when serving fish.

There is a wild variety of fennel—*Foeniculum vulgare*—which, in the Bay Area, commonly grows as a weed along the roadside. This variety has a fibrous, inedible base and stem, but the young finely cut leaves and the seeds can be used as a seasoning. The wild variety can also be added to a charcoal fire, providing a fragrant smoke for barbecuing.

Persimmon

A persimmon is a brilliant-orange, smooth-skinned fruit. An unripe persimmon tastes terrible—astringent and mouth-puckering. A persimmon ripened until it is yieldingly soft is very sweet and succulent. To hasten the ripening of persimmons at home, place them in a paper bag with a few holes pierced in it along with a ripe apple. Persimmons are used for jams, jellies and desserts. They make a superb sherbet.

Holiday Poultry and Game Birds

Flavorful poultry and game birds for the holiday dinner table are difficult to find. Not only should poultry be fresh when purchased, but it should be free of hormones and chemicals. Mass production methods produce two-month old chickens that are the size of Mother Nature's four-month old chickens—unfortunately they still have the same bland, underdeveloped taste of two-month old chickens. The following guide to poultry and game birds available in the Bay Area should help in finding flavorful fowl.

Chickens are raised locally in Petaluma. They are carried fresh by some butchers and many poultry stores.

Ducks are raised locally in Petaluma—especially the white Peking duck. They are available in Chinatown and from many butchers. For quick holiday entertaining, buy a roasted or barbecued duck from a Chinese market.

Geese are raised locally in Sebastopol and Napa. They can be ordered fresh from many butchers beginning in October.

Guinea Hens are available frozen. They have a mildly gamy taste.

Partridges are raised locally in Sonoma County. These fine-tasting game birds usually serve one per person. If you have trouble finding partridges, try Magnani's Poultry in the East Bay—the address is in the Ready Reference—Foods.

Pheasants are raised locally in Sonoma. They have a rich-flavored, somewhat dry meat. One pheasant will feed 2 to 3 people. They are generally available from fall until February.

Quail are raised locally in Hayward. A few markets carry fresh quail in season and a few more will special-order them.

Squab are raised locally in Hayward. A squab is a young pigeon raised especially for eating. Some markets will special-order squab.

Turkeys are raised locally in Sonoma. Hens or toms are considered equally tender. One popular locally raised turkey is the Willie Bird turkey which is available from many butchers and some supermarkets.

Stuffing Poultry

Stuff a bird just before roasting. Contamination occurs when a bird is stuffed and placed in the refrigerator where the cold fails to penetrate the stuffing. Also remember that stuffing expands—fill a bird only three-fourths full.

November Celebrations

Canada Goose

Mountain Man Rendezvous—Felton

There is a living history demonstration of the 1830s and 1840s fur trappers and traders of the American West, including axe-throwing and black powder musket demonstrations at the Roaring Camp and Big Trees Narrow-Gauge Railroad.

Thanksgiving Day—fourth November Thursday

Thanksgiving Day is a day to give thanks for the harvest and for other blessings during the year—it is a federal and legal holiday. The first Thanksgiving Day was observed in the fall of 1621 by the pilgrims of Plymouth Colony. Since then, it has been a day for family gatherings and festive turkey dinners.

Thanksgiving Festival—Mendocino

The festival includes arts, crafts, food, and entertainment.

Harvest Festival—San Francisco

The Harvest Festival is a large festival that travels an annual circuit of western cities. It recreates a nineteenth century American fair and the crafts, foods and drinks, and entertainment are typical of this period. The vendors are costumed.

KQED Wine and Food Festival—San Francisco

Fifty wineries offer a selection of wines and San Francisco's leading restaurants serve a variety of foods from hors d'oeuvres to desserts.

Redwood Empire Jazz Festival—Rohnert Park

Under the supervision of Sonoma State University, 60 junior and senior high school jazz bands and combos compete at the Redwood Empire Jazz Festival. There is also a guest artist noon concert.

University of California and Stanford University Football Game

Traditionally on the eve of the "big game" the two rival university bands parade through the lobbies of leading San Francisco hotels banging their big bass drums. The football game alternates between Berkeley campus and Stanford campus.

Potter's Show and Sale—San Francisco

The Potter's Show and Sale is a one day craft fair, held in the Hall of Flowers in Golden Gate Park. It is sponsored by the Association of San Francisco Potters and Glassblowers. Admission is free.

Christmas at Dunsmuir—Oakland

Dunsmuir is an elaborate turn-of-the-century mansion in a large park-like setting. At the end of November and the beginning of December the grounds are decorated and antiques and crafts are sold.

Holiday Faire and Christmas Lane—San Jose

The Holiday Faire occurs the last weekend of November and the first weekend of December at the Santa Clara County Fairgrounds. The faire features both commercial and non-commercial gift items, craft demonstrations, a children's toy lane and entertainment.

Holleyberry Faire—Geyserville

The Holleyberry Faire is held in the Souverain Winery which is gaily decorated and serves wine while shoppers wander among a selection of hand-crafted items. Holiday food is featured in the winery's restaurant, and there is a gourmet fast food section.

Clocktower Crafts Show—Benicia

The Clocktower Crafts Show is set in an old historical building. It offers a wide variety of holiday and gift items.

Remember the days, even the month, of events may change from year to year. For details see the Ready Reference—Celebrations & Outings.

November Outings

The Sonoma Coast

For those unwilling to hibernate for the winter, a trip 70 miles north of San Francisco to the rugged Sonoma Coast is an invigorating November outing. The deserted Sonoma beaches provide an excellent opportunity to observe coastal birds. Nearly 300 species of birds have been listed for this area.

Bodega Bay

Bodega Bay is the coastal town adjacent to the Sonoma Coast State Beach. Bodega Bay was once a Russian settlement called Kuskoff. Ivan Alexander Kuskoff was an agent for the Russian American Fur Company chartered by Catherine the Great in 1796. Bodega Bay is now a fishing village. In the summer, the harbor contains over 500 commercial fishing boats. There are fewer boats during the winter—but enough boats remain to make the harbor picturesque.

Sonoma Coast State Beach

Just beyond Bodega Bay is the Sonoma Coast State Beach. The beach is actually a series of beaches extending over 13 miles of secluded coves, natural arches, rugged headlands, and craggy coastline. A map of the beaches is available from the Bodega Dunes entrance station or from the park headquarters on Salmon Creek Lagoon. Shell Beach has interesting tidal pools (see August outings on tidal pools). Goat Rock Beach has a particularly scenic shoreline.

All the beaches have beautiful, dramatic surf. The beautiful surf is also dangerous. Extra large, powerful waves called "sleepers" sometimes slam into the shore without warning. These giant waves roll far up the beaches, occasionally knocking down beachcombers and dragging them back into the turbulent surf. Additionally, there is a strong backwash of returning wave water down the steep slope of the beaches—it can sweep you off your feet. And there are also rip currents which can carry the luckless far out to sea.

Needless to say, stay out of the surf. Be alert and careful when strolling the beaches. There are plenty of safe areas to observe both the birds and the surf.

Consult the Ready Reference—Celebrations & Outings (Sonoma Coast) for additional information.

Cormorants

Shoreline Birds

The Sonoma Coast provides an opportunity to observe shoreline birds. Four birds common to the Bay Area as well as the coast are illustrated above and on the following pages.

Cormorant. The cormorant is a dark, beautiful bird frequently sighted in the Bay Area. They are such fine fish catchers that Indian, Chinese, and Japanese fishermen leash them and send them overboard with rings around their throats to prevent them from swallowing their catch. Their reward is every fifth fish. Their inner feathers are not waterproof and you often see them spread out their wings to dry.

November Outings

Gulls

Pelican

Coots

Gull. Surprise, this bird is not a "seagull," but a gull. There are 43 species of gulls. Basically scavengers, they will eat almost anything—once gulls endeared themselves to the citizens of Utah by devouring a locust plague. Their long narrow wings allow them to soar with uncommon grace.

Pelican. The large pelican is fascinating to watch—it flies over the water then dives abruptly with an astonishing speed. It actually hits the water with such impact it stuns the fish. The pelican's lower bill has a huge distensible pouch which it fills with its catch. The brown pelican with a 6½ foot wing span inhabits the Bay Area and the coast. The white pelican with a 10 foot wing span prefers inland lakes.

Coot (mud hen). The coot resembles a duck. It waddles rapidly along the shore. It is amusing to watch. When disturbed it runs laboriously, flapping its stubby wings, puff, puff, ...oh well, a backward glance reassures the coot it has outrun its danger, and it continues pecking its way up the shoreline.

November Outings

Pacific Grove

Pacific Grove is a resort community located 120 miles south of San Francisco that calls itself "Butterfly Town." Its scenic coastline and monarch butterfly phenomenon make it a casual November outing when the weather appears trustworthy. This outing combines well with a visit to nearby Carmel (see October outings) or nearby Cannery Row (see March outings—Monterey).

Ocean View Boulevard

Hugging the coastline in Pacific Grove, Ocean View Boulevard is a scenic rival to the nearby 17-Mile Drive—a healthy entrance fee is charged to view the houses, golf-courses, and coastline along the 17-Mile Drive. The drive along Ocean View Boulevard is free. It begins at Point Aulon or Lovers' Point. The point was originally called Lovers of Jesus Point when Methodist ministers founded the town as a retreat. During the summer it is possible to tour this point in a glass bottomed boat—the world famous marine life of the Pacific Grove area brings renowned scientists to adjacent Hopkins Marine Station.

Pacific Grove Museum

The museum, located at Forest and Central, has been awarded the highest rating for its size of any museum in the United States. Here you can learn about the monarch butterfly as well as about Indian and marine life of Pacific Grove. The submarine canyon in Monterey Bay is comparable to the Grand Canyon.

Where to Find the Butterflies

In October, monarch butterfly "scouts" arrive and some weeks later millions of monarchs arrive for the winter. The City of Pacific Grove welcomes them with a non-commercial—no floats or advertisements—Butterfly Parade of several thousand costumed children.

The trees adjacent to the Milar Butterfly Grove Motel, located at 1073 Lighthouse Avenue, contain dense clusters of butterflies. The motel extends an open invitation to the public to visit the butterflies clustered in the trees on its property.

Washington Park, bordered by Sinex, Short, Alder, and Melrose Streets, is another winter home of many monarchs. Look for them in the underdeveloped section of the park.

Monarch Butterfly

Monarch butterfly is the common name given to the milkweed butterfly, *Danaus plexippus*. The migration of these beautiful orange and black butterflies is still something of a mystery. They migrate from as far away as Alaska and the Canadian Rockies. But since a monarch butterfly's lifespan is less than a year, no monarch butterfly survives to make the journey a second time. Yet the offspring return unguided to winter in the same areas occupied by their parents the previous year.

The beautiful coloring of the monarch butterfly is a protective mechanism. Because their larvae feed on milkweed they have a body juice which is acrid and distasteful to predators. An entirely different butterfly, the viceroy (*Limenitis archippus*) mimics the monarch's coloration and survives by fooling predators who think it is also foul tasting.

The monarch butterfly is common throughout the Bay Area. Hikers sometimes see them clustered on the lower slopes of Mt. Tamalpais. They are often found swarming in the willows bordering the parking lot at Stinson Beach. Natural Bridges State Beach in Santa Cruz has an area where they may be observed from November through February.

For details on outings consult the Ready Reference—Celebrations & Outings (Pacific Grove).

November Outings

Klamath Basin National Wildlife Refuges

Located in the northeast corner of California—astride the Pacific Flyway—the Klamath Basin National Wildlife Refuges attract an estimated 10 million birds during the fall migration. Two of the refuges—Tule Lake Refuge and the Lower Klamath Refuge—have among the greatest concentrations of wildfowl in North America.

Geese

The most prominent of the wildfowl are the geese—early November is prime time for viewing them, particularly the snow geese flying south from the Canadian and Siberian Arctic. There are several other geese species at the refuges including the large gray-brown Canada goose which is illustrated on the November cover page. If your timing is right, what you witness at the refuges may haunt you. Imagine a hundred thousand geese passing between you and the sun. The sky grows dark, and the cacophony—the powerful beating of wings against the air and the wild incessant honking—becomes, as legend has it, a noise to drive men mad.

Shorebirds, Ducks, and Eagles

Many shorebirds also come to the refuges, such as sandhill cranes in flocks as large as anywhere in the world, grebes, Caspaian terns, great blue herons, American egrets, and double-breasted cormorants. Plus there are millions of ducks such as pintails, canvas backs, teals, shovelers, and scaups. Finally when the lake freezes, over 500 bald eagles come down from Alaska to prey upon the water fowl.

Tour Routes

There are auto tour routes through the refuges and a canoe tour route on upper Klamath Lake. Stop in at the refuge headquarters on Hill Road to pick up a brochure and map and have refuge personnel advise where to look for migrating birds.

Lava Bed National Monument

Nearby is the Lava Bed National Monument which is famous for its high cinder cones and subterranean lava caves. Strong flashlights can be borrowed, free, from the Visitor's Center for self-guided cave exploration. Mushpot Cave is outfitted with interpretive signs. Inside the other caves you are free to wander among vivid green mosses, chilling ice flows, and ribbon "lava icicles."

December

Christmas Tree Farm

December Gardening

In Bloom

Annuals: calendula, Iceland poppy, pansy, and sweet alyssum
Perennials: cyclamen, primrose, and violet
Shrubs: azalea and camellia
Early blooming bulbs
Poinsettia

December nights can be quite cold. Be prepared to protect frost-sensitive plants like bougainvillea, citrus, fuchsia, and succulents. See January gardening for specific ideas on frost protection.

Dormant Sprays

December is the first month to apply a dormant spray to deciduous spring flowering fruit trees and rose bushes. Apply dormant spray only after the leaves have fallen. Spray again in January and February. Lime sulfur with oil, and copper oil are considered environmentally safe sprays. They are not chemical insecticides. Dormant sprays are effective against aphids, red spiders, mealy bugs, fungus spores, and scale insects that lay eggs on tree bark. See January gardening for more details on dormant sprays.

Caring for Gift Plants

Azalea. A bright-flowered azalea does not enjoy house visits. While inside place an azalea in a cool spot away from heat sources and keep its soil damp but not soggy. Mist it lightly with water.

Jade plant (*Crassula argentea*). A jade plant is a sturdy succulent—easy to care for, indoors or in the garden. It needs lots of sunshine to bloom well. Plant it anywhere and protect it from frost.

Cyclamen. A cyclamen is an outdoor plant that is intolerant of house heat. While indoors, keep it moist, not soggy, and mist it with water.

Christmas cactus (*Schlumbergera bridgesii*). A Christmas cactus would be miserable in the desert. A native of the tropics, it thrives indoors. Plant it in rich moist soil and fertilize it frequently.

Poinsettia (*Euphorbia pulcherrima*). A poinsettia is probably *the* Christmas plant. While indoors, place a poinsettia in a sunny spot and water it weekly. Do not place a poinsettia in a drafty area or keep its soil constantly wet.

In the Nursery look for:

Annuals: calendula, Iceland poppy, and pansy
Perennials: campanula, cineraria, cyclamen, primrose, and violet
Shrubs: azalea and camellia
Spring blooming bulbs, corms, tubers, and rhizomes
End of December: bare-root plants

December is the last month for digging in bulbs. Wet soil is difficult to dig properly. Be careful not to plant the bulbs too deep. See October gardening for more information on planting bulbs.

Gardening Gifts

To please a gardener (yourself included, of course) give a membership in one of the many horticultural organizations listed on pages 176 to 188. Most of the groups have fascinating newsletters. They are also a terrific way to obtain new and unusual plants from other members.

Buying a Living Christmas Tree

Fir (*Abies*). Most firs have a high mortality rate as living Christmas trees in the Bay Area. Two varieties commonly sold are white fir and noble fir.

Cedar (*Cedrus*). Occasionally the graceful deodar cedar is sold as a living Christmas tree.

Spruce (*Picea*). Spruce is both the most widely sold and the most successful as a living Christmas tree. The varieties of spruce most often sold as living Christmas trees are: Norway spruce, Alberta spruce, Colorado spruce, and Black Hill spruce.

Pine (*Pinus*). The two varieties of pine most often sold as living Christmas trees are Monterey pine and Scotch pine. Both do well.

Native Iris

In December (and the early months of the new year) some species of Pacific Coast iris are sold in nurseries. Native irises are rather new nursery plants so not all nurseries carry them—the irises that are sold are often cultivars with striking blooms. Generally native irises prefer light shade and soil that drains well. They are drought-tolerant once established and will often naturalize to create a striking, easy-to-care-for ground cover. See the illustration on page 45.

December Foods

Cranberries

Cranberries are shiny red, hard berries with a tart, slightly bitter flavor. They are so easy to cook into a sauce it is a shame to buy canned cranberry sauce. To make cranberry sauce bring 1 cup of sugar and 1 cup of water to a boil in a large pan, stirring until the sugar is dissolved. Then add about 3 cups of washed cranberries and cook about five minutes until the berries are translucent and all the skins have popped. That is it—1 quart of cranberry sauce. Flavor cranberries with grated orange rind, or nutmeg while cooking.

Belon Oysters

Belon oysters are fine-tasting, flat, delicate oysters which are aquacultured in Tomales Bay and in Moss Landing. Because they are ideal for eating on the half shell, fish markets carry them during the holiday season. Oysters taste better in winter. They spawn during the summer—during winter they tend to be plumper and less watery.

Zinfandel Nouveau

Zinfandel Nouveau is a wine produced from recently harvested zinfandel grapes. It is a fruity wine and it is meant to be drunk young. Zinfandel has been described as "California Beaujolais"—the Zinfandel Nouveau follows the French tradition of a Beaujolais Nouveau.

Winter Squash

Winter squashes have a hard rind and firm, fibrous flesh—examples of winter squashes are acorn, buttercup, butternut, hubbard, pumpkin, spaghetti, and turban. They are baked like potatoes until tender. All are bland tasting. Cook them to enjoy their texture and color. Flavor winter squash with what will complement your meal such as sweet butter, brown sugar, and grated nutmeg topped with sesame, poppy or caraway seeds; or *crème fraîche* with grated orange rind or minced, fresh ginger; or cheeses melted with chopped scallions and garlic butter.

Butcher Shop Holiday Specialties

Butcher shops often carry holiday specialties such as boned turkey stuffed with sausage or ham and spinach, Swedish ham (*uleskinka*), and Norwegian smoked leg of lamb (*fenalaar*). Italian and German butchers often sell Christmas sausages mixed with cheese and nuts.

Holiday Sweets

The following is a brief guide to some of the holiday sweets available in the greater Bay Area. The Ready Reference—Foods (holiday sweets) lists some of the bakeries, candy makers, and pastry shops that offer seasonal treats.

Traditional American Treats

Fruitcake is usually a buttercake that is baked with candied fruits and nuts. To flavor a fruitcake with liquor, puncture it lightly and pour on warm brandy or wine. Then bury the soaked cake in powdered sugar and age, tightly covered, in a cool, dark place.

Gingerbread men are cookies flavored with ginger and shaped like people. They usually have hair and buttons made with icing.

Mincemeat pie. The mincemeat in a mincemeat pie is basically chopped apples, beef, raisins, and sugar combined with spices and brandy.

Plum pudding is a pudding made with raisins, candied fruit, nuts, eggs, and brandy. It is usually baked in a dish.

Candy. Candy shops sell fudge, divinity, penuche, chocolate molded into holiday shapes, and marzipan, shaped and colored like tiny fruits.

European Treats

Bûche de Noël is an expensive, but gorgeous cake shaped like a log and sometimes decorated with meringue mushrooms. There is usually a choice of fillings and icings.

Stollen is a rich yeast bread that is baked with raisins, citrons, and nuts.

Gâteau St. Honoré is an elaborate cake composed of rings of carmel-glazed, filled cream puffs.

Linzertorte is a luscious dessert pastry that resembles a jam pie. It is usually raspberry flavored.

Panettone is an Italian holiday bread. It is slightly sweet and contains bits of candied fruit and nuts.

Greek krystopsomo is similar to panettone, but it contains a hidden coin to bring the receiver good luck in the new year.

Weihnachtsgeback means Christmas baking. It includes *lebkuchen* (honey bar cookies), *pfeffernusse* (spiced cookie balls rolled in powdered sugar), *springerle* (German anise cookies) and *speculatus* (Dutch molded butter cookies).

December Celebrations

Mountain Winter

Yuletide at Montalvo—Saratoga

During the first three weekends in December, elegant Christmas trees and handcrafted gift items are displayed and sold at Villa Montalvo.

An Elegant Celebration of Christmas—San Francisco

Approximately 80 elegantly decorated Christmas trees and opulent table settings are displayed in a fantasy environment to benefit the American Conservatory Theater. There is also food and a boutique.

Dickens Fair—location varies

The Dickens Fair re-creates a village in the 1800s. Costumed vendors sell food and wares typical of the period. Jugglers, puppeteers, Punch and Judy shows, dancers, and singers provide entertainment. Characters from Charles Dickens's books such as Tiny Tim and Scrooge stroll through the village.

Christmas in Union Square—San Francisco

In December the 16 yew trees in Union Square are lighted and hundreds of poinsettias decorate the paths. From mid-December there is entertainment and a Santa Claus in the square.

Folk Art International—San Francisco

For several weeks a wide variety of folk arts from all over the world are displayed and sold at Folk Art International located at Fort Mason. There are also lectures and films on folk arts.

Mochi Pounding Ceremony—San Francisco

The Mochi Pounding Ceremony is held at the Japan Center on a Sunday in the latter part of December. Japanese Taiko drummers and professional mochi pounders join volunteers in the ceremony which culminates in the making of rice cakes which signify good fortune.

The Nutcracker Ballet—Bay Area

The Nutcracker ballet is performed all over the Bay Area including:
   San Francisco Ballet—San Francisco
   Oakland Ballet—Oakland
   Peninsula Ballet Theater—San Mateo
   Berkeley Conservatory Ballet—Berkeley
   Marin Civic Ballet—San Rafael
   San Jose Dance Theater—San Jose

Handel's *Messiah*—Bay Area

Handel's *Messiah* is performed throughout the Bay Area including:
   Sing-along—San Jose
   Sing-along—San Francisco
   Choir with symphony strings—San Francisco
   Community chorus with orchestra—Oakland
   Symphony orchestra and chorus—San Francisco

New Year's Eve—December 31

New Year's Eve is characterized by festive celebrations to bring in the New Year at midnight.

Remember the day, even the month, of an event may change. For details see the Ready Reference—Celebrations & Outings.

December Outings

Christmas Tree Farms

There are many Christmas tree farms in the greater Bay Area. Some Christmas tree farms provide extras such as picnic tables, free train rides, sleigh rides, tractor rides, and candy canes.

For residents of San Jose and the peninsula there are tree farms in Aptos, Los Gatos, Menlo Park, and Santa Cruz. For Marin County residents, there are tree farms in Napa and Sonoma counties, particularly near Healdsburg. East Bay residents can cut trees in the area near Sunol.

How to Find the Farms

In December newspapers often list Bay Area Christmas tree farms. The harvest guides listed in the Ready Reference—Celebrations and Outings (harvest guides) list Christmas tree farms, and the address of the California Christmas Tree Growers Association, which prints a free list of Christmas tree farms annually.

At the Farms

Tree farms vary considerably in prices for trees—phone them first for prices and directions. Some farms cut the tree for you, others provide you with a saw or ax. Most tree farms bundle trees in a plastic net or overwrap them snugly with twine which reduces the bulk of the tree considerably and protects the tree from needle evaporation at highway speeds. Some tree farms charge modestly for this service, with others it is free.

At Home

The following procedures will help prolong the fresh green quality of a Christmas tree by preventing moisture evaporation.

① Recut the tree one inch or more above the old cut and plunge the trunk immediately into lukewarm water. Keep it in a bucket of water outside until you are ready to decorate.

② Protect the tree from heat. Turn down the heat at night. Turn off the Christmas tree lights when you are not in the room. Mist the tree lightly with water with the Christmas tree lights off.

③ Use a commercial preservative; they are proven to be effective in keeping trees moist. Keep the tree stand reservoir full. Always use a tree stand with a water basin.

Holiday Decorations in San Francisco

The holiday decorations in San Francisco provide a pleasurable although crowded December outing. The most famous store decorations are centered around Union Square.

Decorations in Golden Gate Park

San Francisco's official Christmas tree is the towering Monterey cypress near McLaren Lodge located at the Fell Street park entrance. After viewing the Christmas tree visit the Conservatory of Flowers, which is the oldest building in the park. The elaborate Victorian glass conservatory was shipped around Cape Horn well before the turn of the century. In December it is decorated with an abundance of poinsettias. Also at Golden Gate Park, the Morrison Planetarium located within the California Academy of Sciences, presents a special December show under its 65-foot dome.

Decorations in Stores and Hotels

Many San Francisco stores are legendary for their holiday displays—some of them are listed below.

Gump's (also known as S. G. Gump & Company) is located at 250 Post. The store is known for its Oriental wares—particularly the display of jade in the Jade Room. The window displays at Gumps are usually exceptional. In December crowds gather before the windows, which display animated marionettes in Christmas settings.

Podesta Baldocchi, one of San Francisco's most prestigious flower shops, is located at 224 Grant Avenue. It is turned into a winter fantasyland in December with unusual flower and elaborate ornament displays.

Neiman Marcus is located at the corner of Stockton Street and Geary Street. The elegant store is a branch of the famous Texas store. It incorporated the immense glass dome that was the central feature of the old City of Paris department store. The Christmas displays under the dome are always beautiful.

The **Hyatt Regency** is located at 5 Embarcadero. This hotel has won awards for its atrium lobby which is 20 stories high. The atrium is decorated with plants, trees, a reflecting pool, sculpture, and architectural seating. In December the Christmas display in the atrium is usually innovative and striking.

December Outings

Holiday Performances

Every December there are performances of *The Nutcracker* ballet and stage productions of *A Christmas Carol* throughout the greater Bay Area. Every December also brings Bay Area choir performances—particularly of Middle Ages and Renaissance music. Additionally from Mendocino to Davis to San Jose there are annual choral and orchestral productions of Handel's *Messiah*.

Handel's Messiah

George Frederick Handel (1685–1759) was a composer of Italian operas, but he is most famous for his English oratorios. An oratorio is a musical composition which includes both voices and orchestra and tells a sacred story. The *Messiah* is probably the greatest oratorio ever written. Through alternation of recitatives, arias and choruses, it tells the birth, passion, and triumph of Jesus. In December there are many performances of the *Messiah* in the Bay Area—some are staged with baroque settings and costumes, others are community sing-alongs.

Choir Music

Every mid-December there is a Christmas concert sung by the Cathedral Choir of Boys and Men at Grace Cathedral in San Francisco (Episcopalian). It is so popular that every seat in the Gothic church is filled an hour before it begins.

In San Rafael and San Jose there are choir performances known as singing Christmas trees. These performances present traditional holiday music sung by a large choir which is arranged in a tiered scaffolding shaped like a gigantic, decorated Christmas tree.

Wandering Musicians

Ghirardelli Square in San Francisco has a long standing policy of providing a platform for public entertainment in the square. During December holiday music is performed for free (donations appreciated). The information booth in Ghirardelli Square Plaza lists when the singers and musicians will perform. Pier 39 in San Francisco also has a policy of providing free public entertainment.

See the Ready Reference—Celebrations & Outings (under individual headings) for more details.

The Nutcracker Ballet

The Nutcracker ballet is an extravagant ballet so loved by audiences that it is performed every December. It was written by Piotr Ilich Tchaikovsky (1840-1893). Tchaikovsky is known for his romantic music and theatrical pieces—some critics consider Tchaikovsky the greatest of all Russian composers. The ballet was based on a story by E.T.A. Hoffmann. It was first performed in St. Petersburg, Russia in 1892.

Productions

The two local companies best known for *The Nutcracker* ballet are the San Francisco Ballet and the Oakland Ballet—both offer lavish productions with orchestra. The San Francisco Ballet's *Nutcracker* is usually dramatic and theatrical, while the Oakland Ballet's performance is often soft and dream-like. Other local companies perform *The Nutcracker* in Berkeley, Cupertino, Palo Alto, San Jose, San Mateo, and San Rafael.

A Christmas Carol

Charles Dickens's *A Christmas Carol* is one of the best loved Christmas stories. It is traditionally read at Christmas time. It is also produced on stage, and it has been made into countless movie versions.

Charles Dickens (1812–1870) wrote *A Christmas Carol* as a Christmas book in 1843—partly to make up for financial losses. Dickens was no stranger to debt. The poor family of *A Christmas Carol* was reminiscent of his own impoverished youth. At age 12 Charles Dickens lived alone, supporting himself while his father was confined to a debtors' prison.

Productions

The American Conservatory Theater in San Francisco and other Bay Area groups stage *A Christmas Carol* every year during December.

Of all the movie versions, the 1951 British version with Alistair Sim as Scrooge is considered by many critics to be the best. In 1971 it was made into an average musical starring Albert Finney—the movie was titled *Scrooge*. Movie versions date back to 1908.

Consult the Ready Reference—Celebrations & Outings (Nutcracker Ballet) for companies performing the ballet.

Gardening Update

Bay Area Gardening Groups

With the increased popularity of gardening in the United States, gardeners in the 1990s have many resources to help them increase their skills and enhance their awareness of the seasonal nature of Bay Area living. The following is a brief overview of the public gardens and gardening associations thriving in the greater San Francisco Bay Area.

Membership in several organizations includes a subscription to *Pacific Horticulture*. This quarterly magazine features fine writing combined with good photography and botanical drawings. Subscriptions are available for a modest annual fee. Write *Pacific Horticulture*, P.O. Box 680, Berkeley, CA 94701.

There are several fine gardens in the Bay Area where visitors can see many kinds of plants—Strybing Arboretum in Golden Gate Park, the University of California Botanical Garden in Berkeley, Tilden Park Botanic Garden in Berkeley, and Filoli in Woodside. Each has a program of lectures and activities and an active volunteer program.

Strybing Arboretum specializes in plants from climates similar to San Francisco's. The seventy-acre arboretum is divided into geographical regions plus specialized gardens such as the garden of fragrance and textures for the blind. A favorite of visitors is the cool, dense redwood grove, which features banks of ferns and sorrel as well as the tall, stately redwoods. The New World Cloud Forest is as ethereal as the name implies—situated on a steep hillside, the paths in this section twist among vine-covered trees and plants rescued from the cloud-hugging mountains of the Mexican state of Chiapas. The Strybing Arboretum Society offers lectures, workshops and tours. Membership in the Society brings discounts to the various activities, including plant sales and a subscription to *Pacific Horticulture* magazine. Lectures and talks cover topics such as oaks of the world, climbers and creepers in the garden, or plant collecting in Africa. The fee for non-members is modest. Workshops range from beginning classes in basic gardening to pruning, botanical drawing, or landscape design. Fees for workshops vary. Strybing also offers tours by chartered bus to gardens, growers, and specialized collections. Tours require advance registration. Priority is given to members, and tours fill up fast.

Strybing Arboretum is located just inside the entrance to Golden Gate Park at 9th Avenue and Lincoln Way, San Francisco. Admission is free. Docent-led tours are available. Open 8:00 A.M. to 4:30 P.M. weekdays, 10:00 A.M. to 5:00 P.M. weekends and holidays. For more information on the programs available call (415) 661-0668.

The **University of California Botanical Garden** in Berkeley contains one of the largest collections of plants in America. The 33 acres are organized by geographical regions such as Africa, Japan, and New Zealand. The hilly setting offers spectacular views of the Golden Gate Bridge plus the soothing sounds of Strawberry Creek, which meanders through the gardens forming a series of cascades and waterfalls. There is a large cactus garden and an extensive collection of herbs, which includes a new Chinese herbal section with plants intriguingly labeled according to remedy.

Friends of the University of California Botanical Garden sponsor several activities each month such as a symposium on the mixed border or a lecture on Chinese medicinal herbs. Membership includes their quarterly newsletter, discounts on classes, discounts on visitor center purchases, and early admission to their Spring Plant Sale. Write the Botanical Garden, Centennial Drive, University of California, Berkeley CA 94720, or phone (415) 642-2084.

The garden is on Centennial Drive (east of Memorial Stadium in Strawberry Canyon). Admission is free. Docent-led tours available. Open 9:00 A.M. to 4:30 P.M. everyday except Christmas. Phone (415) 642-3343.

The Arboretum at the **University of California at Santa Cruz** also has an active program. The UCSC Arboretum is especially strong in Australian plants and in ornamentals for California gardens such as deer-resistant and drought-resistant plants. Contact the Arboretum Associates, UCSC Arboretum, Santa Cruz, CA 95064.

Also the **University of California at Davis** has an aboretum which specializes in native California plants. Contact the Friends of the Davis Arboretum located on La Rue Road in Davis. Phone (916) 752-2498.

Filoli is the Georgian-style country mansion and estate garden located on the Peninsula. There are 17 acres of formal year-round floral display gardens. House and garden tours (admission fee charged) are held from mid-February to mid-November. Reservations are required. Friends of Filoli sponsor a wide range of events from practical workshops on wisteria pruning and tool sharpening to outright socials such as opera recitals and tea dances. Both a bridge tournament and a tour of England's Chelsea Flower Show were offered in a recent newsletter. Membership includes four free docent-led tours, non-transferable, by reservation, a bimonthly newsletter, four free Friends Days, and priority in purchasing tickets for events at Filoli. Write the Friends of Filoli at Cañada Road, Woodside CA 94062, or phone (415) 364-2880.

Gardening Update

Another highly regarded garden is the East Bay Regional Park District's **Tilden Park Botanic Garden**. Except for the towering non-native eucalyptus, the 2,065-acre Tilden Park seems to have evolved naturally into groves of oaks and open meadows. Both Strybing Arboretum and the U.C. Berkeley Botanical Garden in Berkeley have large native plant sections, but the botanic garden in Tilden Park is devoted exclusively to California plants. The 10-acre site includes over 2,000 native plants arranged by regions in a series of stone terraces bordering a small creek. There is a lecture and slide show on Saturdays from November through February. The visitors center sells seeds and books.

The garden is located in the Berkeley hills on Wildcat Canyon Road near South Park Drive. Open daily (except major holidays) from 10:00 A.M. to 5:00 P.M. Admission is free. Phone (415) 841-8732.

There is no membership association. However, gardeners with a technical nature may wish to subscribe to their quarterly journal *The Four Seasons*, which emphasizes native plants. Write to the Journal of the East Bay Regional Park District, Botanic Garden, Tilden Regional Park, Berkeley CA 94708.

Tilden Park Botanic Garden is supported by volunteers from the local chapter of the **California Native Plant Society**. Native plants are popular right now, and this is a very active group. Most of the action is at the local level; the many chapters offer monthly meetings, native plant sales, and wildflower shows. They also chase after "escaped exotics" such as pampas grass and Scotch broom, which are invading native plant territory. To locate the nearest local chapter and join the CNPS write the state headquarters: California Native Plant Society, 909 12th Street, Suite 116, Sacramento, CA 95814. Membership includes the quarterly journal *Fremontia* (a rather technical publication), the CNPS *Bulletin* (events and issues), and the local chapter newsletter. Native plant societies hold plant sales in fall, usually in October, which is the best time to plant natives.

Gardeners on the Peninsula may wish to join the **Western Horticultural Society**, which meets once a month to hear speakers with a specialized knowledge in some area of horticulture. Unusual plants are brought to the meetings and discussed. The Society also offers field trips. Membership includes a subscription to *Pacific Horticulture* magazine. Write the Society at 746 University Avenue, Los Altos, CA 94022.

There are many garden associations devoted to one type of plant such as irises, roses, or herbs. In addition to the educational and social benefits of belonging to these groups, they are a great way to increase your plants. The following groups are just a sampling of what exists.

A great many plant groups participate in the annual **Flower Show** usually held in August at the San Francisco County Fair Building (right beside Strybing Arboretum) in Golden Gate Park. Many garden associations also participate in the **San Francisco Landscape Garden Show**, which is usually held in April at Pier 3, Fort Mason, San Francisco. Over 200 national horticultural organizations are listed in the recently updated *Gardening By Mail 2: A Source Book* by Barbara Barton. Write Tusker Press, P. O. Box 1338, Sebastopol, CA 95473 for information on ordering this valuable resource book.

The **American Iris Society** is very active locally, partly because there are more iris hybridizers here than in any other region of the world. The iris society is interested in not only the tall bearded irises, but many other species such as Pacific Coast native irises or Japanese irises. Each subgroup has its own bulletin. To join write the American Iris Society, Membership Secretary, 6518 Beachy Avenue, Wichita, Kansas 67206. Membership includes the national quarterly bulletin (100 pages of iris news) and the quarterly regional bulletin. There is a small additional fee for the species sections. New members also receive an attractive, informative booklet on growing irises. The society holds several sales in the Bay Area.

The **American Rose Society** has groups throughout the Bay Area, which hold monthly meetings, social events, and rose shows. To find a local group contact the national headquarters. Membership includes the monthly *American Rose Magazine*. Write the ARS at P. O. Box 30000, Shreveport, LA 71130. Also ask for a list of consulting rosarians in your area who will answer your rose growing questions for free, whether or not you are a member. The San Francisco Chapter has produced a terrific 126-page book titled *Growing Roses in the San Francisco Bay Area*. You may order a copy from the San Francisco Chapter or buy one at their annual rose pruning demonstration held every year in Golden Gate Park in January.

The **Northern California Unit of the Herb Society** of America schedules several activities each month in areas such as culinary, horticultural, craft, and plant study. Membership includes the national herbal newsletter three times a year and the local calendar. For information write the Herb Society of America, 2 Independence Court, Concord MA 01742.

Gardening Update

The **California Rare Fruit Growers** has several local chapters which meet five times a year and hold scion exchanges, field trips and plant sales. The fruits, by the way, are not necessarily rare. This is definitely the group to join to find out what fruits thrive in your area. Write California Rare Fruit Growers, Fullerton Arboretum, California State University, Fullerton, CA 92634.

The **Northern California Daffodil Society** meets four times each year to exchange information and stage an annual daffodil show. The show includes an artistic arrangement class which has a theme such as Daffodil Melodies and entries with titles such as "The Breeze and I." Write the American Daffodil Society Inc., Route 3, 2302 Byhalia Road, Hermando, MS 38632.

The **Western Chapter of the American Rock Garden** Society meets approximately once a month at a member's home or a public garden to hear lectures or hold workshops. The group also schedules field study trips. Write the secretary, Nell Forkman, at 2640 San Benito Drive, Walnut Creek, CA 94598.

There are several munificent groups dedicated to enhancing the public landscape. The **California Nature Conservancy**, headquartered at 785 Market Street, San Francisco, CA 94103 (phone 777-0487) protects rare and endangered native plants, animals, and natural communities. Volunteers protect and care for a wide variety of preserves. The **San Francisco Friends of the Urban Forest**, 512 Second Street, 4th Floor, San Francisco, CA 94107 (phone 543-5000) plants trees in San Francisco to create a livable urban environment.

Finally, this list would be incomplete without mentioning two fine groups located in San Francisco.

The **California Horticultural Society** joins professionals with knowledgable laymen to discuss plants and hear lectures every month at the California Academy of Sciences in Golden Gate Park. Membership includes *Pacific Horticulture* magazine and a monthly bulletin. Write the Society at the California Academy of Sciences, San Francisco, CA 94118.

The **San Francisco League of Urban Gardeners** is a large, very active group which supports community and school gardens (74 gardens currently) plus home gardens, workshops, and educational projects. If you grow vegetables in San Francisco (or want to grow them), join this group. Membership includes discounts on supplies, free advice, an excellent quarterly newsletter and calendar of events. Write SLUG, 2540 Newhall Street, San Francisco, CA 94124.

Of course, many communities also have one or more local garden groups devoted to gardening.

Other Public Gardens

In addition to the gardens discussed above, there are other gardens open to the public in the Bay Area where visitors may witness the seasonal nature of Bay Area living.

Golden Gate Park in San Francisco contains several specialized gardens within its 1,017 acres. The Conservatory of Flowers on Kennedy Drive imitates the grand glass Kew Gardens Conservatory of London. It contains orchids and tropical plants. The Japanese Tea Garden is beautifully landscaped and breathtaking when the cherry trees bloom in spring. A small admission fee is charged for each.

Blake Garden, located at 70 Rincon Road in Kensington, is part of the residence of U.C. Berkeley's president. It offers a fine example of landscape architecture. Open weekdays 8:30 A.M. to 4:30 P.M.

Dunsmuir House and Gardens, located at 2960 Peralta Oaks Court in Oakland (take 580 to 106th Avenue), offers a glimpse of gardening in 1899 with its palm trees, lake, and gazebo. Admission fee charged. Phone 562-0329 for current hours.

Berkeley Rose Garden located one mile north of the university on Euclid Avenue in Berkeley, has 4,000 rose bushes with a superb view of San Francisco Bay. Open dawn to dusk.

Morcom Amphitheater of Roses, located in Oakland on Jean Avenue (take 580 to Grand Avenue), has 5,000 rose bushes arranged grandly in a formal Italian style with stonemasonry and ironwork. Open dawn to dusk.

San Jose Municipal Rose Garden located at Naglee and Dana Avenues in San Jose, has 7,500 rose bushes arranged around a fountain.

Hakone Japanese Garden is discussed on page 44.

Villa Montalvo, located in Saratoga at the end of Montalvo Road contains a garden of California natives typical of the Santa Cruz mountains. Phone (408) 867-0190 for hours.

The Water-Conserving Garden located at the Marin County Civic Center in San Rafael offers many ideas for drought-resistant gardens. The plants are labeled, and there are picnic tables. Unfortunately, it is open only on weekdays.

Western Hills Nursery, located in the hills above Occidental (Sonoma County) at 16250 Coleman Valley Road, is an inspiration to gardeners. A well-worn foot path leads alongside ponds and through rockeries. Phone (707) 874-3731 for current hours.

Ready-Reference

Introduction to the Ready-Reference

There are three separate indexes.
Ready-Reference—Gardening, pages 181–184
Ready-Reference—Foods, pages 185–187
Ready-Reference—Celebrations & Outings, pages 188–199

The Ready-Reference is more than an index. It is an easy-to-read source of information to help the reader quickly reach the telephone numbers and addresses needed to plan an outing or a seasonal activity. A telephone call will make available the latest prices, hours, specific transportation instructions, and weather conditions.

There are additional sources listed in the Ready-Reference that are not mentioned in the text. For example, under the heading camping, there is a telephone number for state campsite information, a telephone number for United States forest camping information, a telephone number for national parks information, and a telephone number for weather conditions in local national parks.

There are many commercial establishments listed in the Ready-Reference. Neither the author nor the publisher endorses these establishments nor believes them to be superior to their competitors. They are listed as a convenience to the reader.

The author would greatly appreciate any information on changes or additions to the Ready-Reference readers feel would add to the pleasure of living in the Bay Area. She may be reached through the publisher— the address is on the last page.

Gardening

A

African daisy, **81**
Artichokes, **5**
Asparagus, **5**
Azaleas, **4**, **17**, **34**, **64**, **106**, **136**, **164**

B

Bare-root planting, **5**, **17**, **19**
Basil, **48**, **123**
Bay, **48**
Begonia, **129**
  sources:
    ❀ Antonelli Brothers Begonias
     2545 Capitola Road
     Santa Cruz
    ❀ Carmel Valley Begonia Gardens
     9920 Carmel Valley Road
     Carmel Valley   ☎ 408/624-7231
Berkeley Rose Garden, **179**
Berries, **18**, **19**, **93**. *See also* specific
  berries
Blackberries, **19**
Blake Garden, **179**
Bougainvillea, **4**, **47**
Bouquet garni, **121**
Bulbs, **17**, **35**, **46**, **123**, **137**, **151**
Bush beans, **67**

C

Calycanthus, **123**
Carpenteria californica, **123**
Camellias, **16**, **17**, **34**, **64**, **106**, **136**, **137**
Cane berries, **4**, **19**
Catalogs, **16**. *See also* Garden catalogs;
  Herb catalogs; Iris catalogs, Wild-
  flower catalogs
Ceanothus, **35**
Cedar, **165**
Cercis occidentalis, **123**
Chives, **48**

Christmas cactus, **164**
Christmas trees, **165**
Chrysanthemums, **4**, **80**, **150**
Citrus, **4**, **6**, **17**
Cotoneaster, **150**
Cucumbers, **67**
Cyclamen, **4**, **164**

D

Daffodil Hill, **39**
Dill, **48**
Dormant Spray, **16**, **164**
Drought-tolerant plants, **35**, **81**, **123**,
  165
Dunsmuir House, **155**, **179**

E

Earwigs, **95**

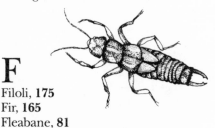

F

Filoli, **175**
Fir, **165**
Fleabane, **81**
Flowers. *See* specific flower
Fortnight lily, **81**
Fremontodendron, **123**
Frost, **4**, **164**
Fruit trees, **4**, **46**, **64**, **93**
Fuchsias, **34**, **46**, **80**

G

Garden catalogs, **16**. *See also*
  Herb catalogs; Iris catalogs, and
  Wildflower catalogs
The following catalogs sell plants,
  trees, and vegetables; the cost of
  each catalog is in parentheses.
  ❀ Anthony J. Skittone
   (unique bulbs, protea—$1)
   1415 Eucalyptus Drive
   San Francisco, CA 94132

Gardening

❀ Bountiful Gardens
(organic vegetables—$1)
5798 Ridgewood Road
Willits, CA 95490

❀ Burpee Seed Company
(large, colorful catalog—free)
300 Park Avenue
Warminster, PA 18974

❀ George W. Park Seed Co.
(large, colorful catalog—free)
S.C. Highway 254 N.
Greenwood, SC 29647

❀ J. L. Hudson, Seedsman
(specializes in the rare,
catalog—$1) P.O. Box 1058
Redwood City, CA 94064

❀ Kitazawa Seed Company
(Asian vegetables)
356 W. Taylor Street
San Jose, CA 95110

❀ Le Marche Seeds.
(gourmet vegetables—$2)
P.0. Box 190
Dixon, CA 95620

❀ Redwood City Seed Co.
(vegetables—$1)
P.O. Box 361
Redwood City, CA 94064

❀ Shepherd's Garden Seeds
(gourmet vegetables—$2)
7389 W. Zayante Road
Felton, CA 95018

❀ Thompson & Morgan
(superb catalog—free)
P.O. Box 1308
Jackson, New Jersey 08527

❀ Van Bourgondien Brothers
(bulbs—free)
P.O. Box A
245 Farmingdale Road, Rt. 109
Babylon, N.Y. 11702

Garlic, **106**
Geraniums, **63**, **65**, **122**
Gladiolus, **4**
Golden shrub daisy, **81**
Grasshoppers, **91**
Gray lavender cotton, **81**

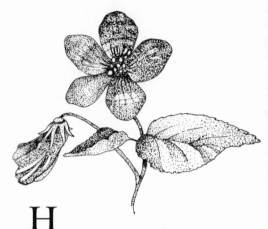

H

Hakone Japanese Garden, **44**
Heavenly bamboo, **150**
Herbs, **47**, **48**, **49**, **123**. *See also*
individual listings
retail gardens:
❀ Saso Herb Gardens
14625 Fruitvale Avenue
Saratoga   ☎408/867-0307
Herb catalogs, **47**
❀ Herb Gatherings, Inc.
(informative catalog $2)
5742 Kenwood
Kansas City, MO 64110
❀ Le Jardin du Gourmet
(inexpensive mini-seed packs
sold—catalog 50 cents)
P.O. Box 44
West Danville, VT 05873
❀ Nichols Garden Nursery
(informative catalog)
1190 Northwest Pacific Highway
Albany, OR 97321
Hydrangeas, **80**, **106**

I

Impatiens, **81**
Insects, **94**, **95**
Iris, **93**, **107**
Iris catalogs, **81**

❀ Bay View Gardens
famous for Pacific Coast hybrids
(catalog—$1)
1201 Bay Street
Santa Cruz CA 95060
❀ Cottage Gardens
(bearded iris, catalog $.50)
6225 Vine Hill School Road
Sebastopol, CA   ☎707/823-3322
❀ Maryott Iris Gardens
(catalog—$1)
1069 Bird Avenue
San Jose CA 95125
☎408/265-2498
❀ Schreiner's Gardens Iris Catalog
(catalog—$2, refundable
with order)
3639 Quinaby
Salem, OR 97303

J

Jade plant, **164**

L

Lavender, **48**
Lawns, **34**, **46**, **122**
Lily, **107**
Liquidambar, **150**
Lobelia, **80**

M

Marin Civic Center Garden, **179**
❀ Marin Art and Garden Center
Sir Francis Drake Boulevard
Ross   ☎415/452-5597
Maple, **150**
Mendocino Botanical Gardens, **73**
Mexican sage, **81**
Mint, **49**, **123**

N

Nasturtium, **49**
Native plants, **35**, **123**, **136**, **165**
nursery:
❀ Yerba Buena
19500 Skyline Boulevard
Woodside   ☎415/851-1668

O

Onions, **106**
Orchids, **38**
plant sources:
❀ John Ewing Orchids
287 White Road
Watsonville   ☎408/684-1111
❀ Orchid Garden Nursery
33 Los Robles Drive
Carmel Valley   ☎408/659-3940
❀ Rod McLellan's Orchid Nursery
1450 El Camino Real
South San Francisco
☎415/871-5655
Oregano, **49**
Organizations, **176–181**

P

Parsley, **49**, **123**
Pests, **94**, **95**
Pine, **165**
Poinsettia, **4**, **164**
Primroses, **17**
Pruning, **64**
Pumpkin, **135**, **140**, **142**, **143**

R

Radishes, **67**
Raspberries, **19**, **79**
Rhododendron, **17**, **64**, **65**, **106**

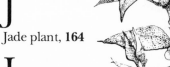

Gardening

Romneya coulteri, **121**
Rosemary, **49**
Roses
  general care, **34, 64, 80, 136**
  ailments, **64**
  pruning, **4**
  varieties recommended, **5**
  gardens:
    Berkeley, **179**
    Oakland, **179**
    San Jose, **179**
    San Francisco, **9**
  retail sources:
  ● Garden Valley Ranch
    498 Pepper Road
    Petaluma   ☎707/795-0919
  ● John's Rose Garden
    1020 Mt. George Avenue
    Napa   ☎707/224-8002
  ● Roses of Yesterday and Today
    802 Brown's Valley Road
    Watsonville   ☎408/724-2755

S

Sage, **49, 123**
San Jose Rose Garden, **179**
Sea lavender, **81**
Shasta daisies, **17, 122**
Slugs, **16, 34, 64, 95**
Snails, **16, 34, 64, 95**
Sorrel, **49**
Spearmint, **49, 123**
Spruce, **165**
Strybing Arboretum, **174**
Strawberries, **18**
Sweet alyssum, **80**
Sweet marjoram, **49**

T

Tarragon, **49**
Tilden Park Botanic Garden, **176**
Thyme, **49**
Tomatoes, **66, 67**
Tuberous begonias, **136**

U

University of California
  Berkeley Botanic Garden, **175**
  Davis Arboretum, **175**
  Santa Cruz Arboretum, **175**

V

Vegetables, **47, 66, 67**
  See also specific vegetables
Villa Montalvo, **44, 161, 179**

W

Western Hills Nursery, **179**
Wildflowers, **151**
Wildflower catalogs, **151**
  ● Clyde Robin Seed Co.
    (catalog—$2)
    P. O. Box 2366
    Castro Valley, CA 94546
                    ☎415/581-3468
  ● Larner Seeds
    (catalog—$1)
    P. O. Box 407
    235 Fern Road
    Bolinas, CA 94924

Z

Zucchini, **67**

Foods

A

Abalone, **37**
Apple, **138**
Apricot, **82**
Arugula, **50**
Artichoke, **7**
Asparagus, **36**
Avocado, **20**

B

Bakeries, **51**
Basil, **48**, **127**
Bean curd, **21**
Bean sprouts, **21**
Belon oyster, **166**
Berries, **83**
Blueberry, **83**
Bread, **51**
Bok choy, **21**
Bouquet garni, **121**, **126**
Boysenberry, **83**

C

Cabbage, **152**
Cantaloupe, **97**
Cardoon, **7**
Casaba melon, **97**
Compound butter, **126**
Cheese, **109**
   The following is a sample of Bay
     Area cheese makers
   🐂 Marin French Cheese Company
     7500 Red Hill Road
     (D Street extension)
     Petaluma, CA 94952
          ☎707/762-6001
   🐂 Sonoma Cheese Factory
     2 Spain Street
     Sonoma, CA 95476
          ☎707/996-1000

   🐂 Vella Cheese Company
     315 Second St. East
     Sonoma, CA 95476
          ☎707/938-3232
Cherry, **82**
Chestnut, **152**
Chevre, **109**
Chicken, **153**
Chinese parsley, **21**
Chinese vegetables, **21**
Chives, **48**, **127**
Cilantro, **21**
Clam, **37**
Coriander, **21**
Crab, **37**
Cranberry, **166**
Crayfish, **37**. *See also* Delta crayfish
Crème fraîche, **107**
Crenshaw melon, **97**

D

Dandelion greens, **36**
Delta crayfish, **37**
   From May through October cray-
     fish may be purchased live.
   🐂 Delta Crayfish
     608 Highway 12
     Rio Vista, CA 94571
          ☎707/374-6654
Dill, **48**, **126**
Dim sum, **13**. *See also* Ready Reference
   —Celebrations & Outings
   (Chinatown)
Duck, **153**

E

Eggplant, **96**

F

Fennel, **152**
Fig, **108**
Fish, **69**

Foods

G

Garlic, **124**
Ginger root, **21**
Goose, **153**
Grape, **124**
Green beans (haricots verts), **82**
Guinea hen, **153**

H

Halibut, **69**
Haricots verts, **82**
Herbs, **126, 127**. *See also* Ready
   Reference—Gardening (herbs)
Herring, **6**
Holiday sweets, **167**
Honeydew melon, **97**

I

Icicle radish, **21**

J

Jam, **83**

L

Late harvest wine, **138**
Lemongrass, **82**
Ling cod, **69**
Lotus root, **21**

M

Mango, **68**
Marin French Cheese Company, **109**
   See also Cheese
Melon, **97**
Mint, **49, 127**
Mung bean sprouts, **21**
Mussels, **37**
Mustard greens, **21**

N

Napa cabbage, **21**
Nasturtium blossom, **138**
Nectarine, **108**
New potato, **50**

O

Ollalieberry, **83**
Onion, **68**
Oregano, **49, 126**
Oriental vegetables, **21**
Oyster, **37, 124, 130, 166**
   ᐓ Jensen's Oyster Beds
      alas, apparently out of buiness
   ᐓ Johnston's Oyster Farm
      P.O. Box 68
      Inverness, CA 94927
                     ☎415/669-1149
   ᐓ Tomales Bay Oyster Co.
      P.O. Box 29
      Point Reyes Station, CA 94956
                     ☎415/663-1242

P

Parsley, **49, 50**
Partridge, **153**
   partridge is available from:
   ᐓ Magnani Poultry
      6317 College Avenue, Oakland
      1556 Hopkins Ave., Berkeley
Peach, **96**
Pear, **108**
Peas, **68, 138**
Persian melon, **97**
Persimmon, **152**
Pesto, **127**
Pheasant, **153**
Poultry, **153**
Prawn, **20**

Q

Quail, **153**

R

Radicchio, **36**
Radish, **82**
Raspberry, **83**
Red snapper, **69**

S

Sablefish, **69**
Salad greens, **6**, **36**, **50**
Salmon, **50**, **69**
Shark, **69**
Shellfish, **6**, **20**, **37**
Shrimp, **20**, **37**
Snow pea, **21**, **50**
Sole, **69**
Sonoma Cheese Factory, **109**
   See also Cheese
Sorrel, **20**, **49**
Squab, **153**
Squid, **37**
Stir-frying, **20**, **21**
Strawberries, **68**, **83**
Sugar snap pea, **68**
Sweet basil, **49**, **127**

T

Tarragon, **49**, **127**
Tea, **127**
Tofu, **21**
Tomato, **97**
Tomatillo, **108**
Trout, **69**
Turkey, **153**

V

Vella Cheese Company, **109**. *See also* Cheese
Vinegar, **126**

W

Watermelon, **97**
Wine, **125**, **138**, **168**

Wineries (Bay Area), **125**
   See also Napa Valley wineries in the Ready Reference—Celebrations and Outings (Napa Valley), and pages **132**, **133**
   ⌘ Takara Sake USA Inc.
      708 Addison Street
      Berkeley, CA 94702
                    ☎415/540-8250
   ⌘ Concannon Vineyards
      4590 Tesla Road
      Livermore, CA 94550
                    ☎415/447-3760
   ⌘ Stony Ridge Winery
      1188 Vineyard Ave.
      Pleasanton, CA 94556
                    ☎415/846-2133
   ⌘ Wente Brothers
      5565 Tesla Road
      Livermore, CA 94550
                    ☎415/447-3603
   ⌘ Paul Masson Champagne & Wine Cellars
      13150 Saratoga Ave.
      Saratoga, CA 95070
                    ☎408/257-7800
   ⌘ Mirassou Vineyards
      3000 Aborn Road
      San Jose, CA 95135
                    ☎408/274-4000
   ⌘ Weibel Champagne Vineyards
      Stanford Ave.
      Mission San Jose, CA 94538
                    ☎415/490-9914
   ⌘ Grand Pacific Vineyards
      341 San Anselmo Ave.
      San Anselmo, CA ☎415/459-5557

Winter salad greens, **6**, **20**, **36**
Winter squash, **166**

Z

Zinfandel Nouveau, **166**
Zucchini blossom, **96**

Celebrations & Outings

A

Aki Matsuri, **129**   ☎408/295-0367
A La Carte, A La Park, **128**
                       ☎415/974-6900
Almaden Valley Festival, **129**
                       ☎408/268-1133
An Elegant Celebration
  of Christmas, **171**   ☎415/771-3880
Angel Island State Park, **134**
                       ☎415/435-1915
  Red & White Fleet carries passen-
  gers between Pier 43½ in San
  Francisco and Angel Island most
  of the year.   ☎415/546-2805
  Angel Island Ferry runs from Tibu-
  ron to Angel Island
                       ☎415/435-2131
  Elephant Train Tours
                       ☎415/435-1915
Angels Camp, **58,71**
Año Nuevo, **24–27**
  ➥Año Nuevo State Reserve
    San Mateo Coast Area
    95 Kelly Avenue
    Half Moon Bay, CA 94019
                       ☎415/879-0227
    Purchase tickets through
    Ticketron   ☎415/974-6391
Apple picking, **144**
Apple Hill Growers Festival, **141**
                       ☎916/626-2344
Armstrong Redwood State Reserve,
  101
Art and Wine Festival (Hayward), **110**
                       ☎415/351-8292
Art and Wine Festival (Novato), **85**
                       ☎415/897-1164
Art Festival (Piedmont), **140**
                       ☎415/420-3000
Art Festival (San Francisco), **84**
        ☎415/558-4888 or 558-3463
Artichoke Festival, **129**
                       ☎408/633-2465
Arts and Crafts Fair (San Bruno), **140**
                       ☎415/588-0180
Auburn, **61**   ☎916/885-5616

Audubon Canyon Ranch, **76**
  ➥4900 Shoreline Highway
    Stinson Beach, CA 94970
                       ☎415/383-1644
August Moon Concerts, **110**
Autumnal equinox, **September 22 or
  23**   ☎707/963-2761

B

Bay to Breakers, **70**
Begonia Festival, **129**
Benicia, **110**, **128**, **145**
Berryessa Art and Wine Festival, **71**
                       ☎408/998-7000
Big Basin Redwoods State Park, **54**
                       ☎408/338-6132
Big Game, **155**
Birds, **149**, **157–159**, **162**
Bodega Bay, **156**
  ➥Chamber of Commerce
    913 Highway 1,
    Bodega Bay, CA 94923
                       ☎707/875-3422
Bon Festival, **99**   ☎415/922-6776
Butterfly, **160–161**
Butterfly Parade, **141**, **160**
                       ☎418/646-6506

C

Calaveras Big Trees State Park, **29**
  ➥P.O. Box 120
    Arnold, CA 95223 ☎209/795-2334
Calaveras Jumping Frog Jubilee,
  58, 71
  ➥P.O. Box 96
    Angels Camp, CA 95222
                       ☎209/736-2561
California holidays, **8**
California Rodeo, **99**   ☎408/757-2951
California sea lion, **15**, **26**
California sea otter, **15**, **26**

Christmas in the Park, **168**
    ☎408/998-7000
Christmas in Union Square, **169**
    ☎415/974-6900
Christmas trees, **170**
  Send a self-addressed, stamped,
  large envelope for a free
  "Choose and Cut" Christmas
  tree guide.
  ➺California Christmas Tree Grow-
  ers, P.O. Box 1752
  Layayette, CA 94549
    ☎415/283-8085
Cinco de Mayo, **70**
  Santa Clara Valley celebrations
    ☎408/998-7000
  San Francisco celebrations
    ☎415/974-6900
Clam Chowder Cookoff, **23**
    ☎408/342-7755
Clocktower Crafts Show, **155**
    ☎707/745-5788
Coloma, **61**
  State Historic Park
    ☎916/622-3470
  ➺Columbia State Historic Park, **58**
  P.O. Box 151   ☎209/532-4301
  Columbia, CA 95310
Columbus Day, **140**   **October12**
  San Francisco celebrations
    ☎415/974-6900
  San Jose celebrations
    ☎408/998-7000
Concord Fall Festival, **128**
Concord Jazz Festival, **110**
  ➺P.O. Box 845   ☎415/671-3270
  Concord, CA 94522
Concours d'Elegance, **71**, **99**, **111**
  ➺Lafayette (July) ☎415/284-7404
  ➺Pebble Beach (August)
    ☎408/649-3200
  ➺Silverado Country Club
    ☎415/652-9202
Coyote Point Museum, **9**
    ☎415/342-7755
Cupertino Art and Wine Festival, **110**
    ☎408/252-7054

D

Daffodil Hill, **39**, **61**
Delta, **102–103**
  Brannan Island has 100 campsites
  reserve through Ticketron
  California Railway Museum, Rio
  Vista   ☎707/374-2978
  Houseboat rentals (more available)
  ➺Herman and Helen's Marina
  Venice Island Ferry Stockton,
  CA 95209   ☎209/951-4634
  ➺Courtland Docks Houseboats
  P.O Box 427   ☎916/775-1360
  Courtland, CA 95615
  ➺King Island Houseboats
  11530 W. 8 Mile Road
  Stockton, CA 95209
    ☎209/478-0210
  Boat cruises
  ➺Channel Star Excursions
    ☎916/441-6481
    ☎800/433-0263
  ➺Delta Travel Agency
  P.O. Box 813   ☎916/372-3690
  West Sacramento, CA 95691
Dickens Fair, **168**
Dim sum, **13**. *See also* Chinatown
Dixieland Jazz Festival, **70**
    ☎916/372-5277
Dog shows, **23**
  San Francisco   ☎415/652-9202
  San Jose   ☎408/257-6400
Dog sled races, **9**, **23**
  McCloud   ☎916/964-2471
  Truckee   ☎916/587-3276
Duxbury Reef, **115**

E

Elephant seals, **24–27**. *See also* Año
Nuevo
Emerald Bay, **116**. *See also* Lake Tahoe

Celebrations & Outings

•❖Friends of the Sea Otter Center
P.O. Box 221220 ☎408/625-3290
Carmel, CA 93922
California State Fair, **111**
☎916/924-2000
Calistoga, **40–41**
•❖Calistoga Chamber of Commerce
P.O. Box 321
Calistoga, CA 94515
☎707/942-6333
Old Faithful Geyser ☎707/942-6463
Silverado Museum (St. Helena)
☎707/963-3757
Sharpsteen Museum ☎707/942-5911
Jack London State Historic Park
☎707/938-5216
Mud baths (most are also motels,
there are more available)
Calistoga Spa ☎707/942-6269
Dr. Wilkinson's Hot Springs
☎707/942-4102
Soaring Center "glider planes"
☎707/942-5592
Camellia Festival, **39** ☎916/442-5542
Campbell Highland Games, **111**
☎408/378-6252
Camping, **54, 57, 73, 74, 87, 90, 101,
102, 116, 130, 133**
State Park Campsite Reservation
Information ☎800/444-7275
National Parks Information
☎415/556-4122
National Parks Parkcast
(weather) ☎415/556-6030
U.S. Forest Maps, Camping
Information ☎415/556-0122
Ticketron ☎415/393-6914
Cannery Row, **42**
Capitola, **90, 129**. *See also* Santa Cruz
•❖Chamber of Commerce
410 Capitola Avenue
Capitola, CA 95010
☎408/475-6522
•❖Antonelli Begonia Gardens
2545 Capitola Road
Capitola, CA 95010
☎408/475-6522

Carmel, **98, 146**
•❖Business Association
P.O. Box 4444 ☎408/624-2522
Carmel-by-the-Sea, CA 93921
•❖Bach Festival
P.O. Box 575 ☎408/624-1521
Carmel-by-the Sea, CA 93921
Carmel Mission ☎408/624-1271
•❖Pt. Lobos Reserve Park
Route 1, Box 62
Carmel, CA 93923 ☎408/624-4909
Carnival San Francisco, **52**
☎415/974-6900
Castro Street Fair, **140**
☎415/346-2640
Castro Valley, **129**
Cat Show, **23** ☎707/584-5862
Charmarita, **70** ☎415/726-5202
Cherry Blossom Festival, **53**
☎415/922-6776
Cherry trees blooming, **39**
Chinatown (San Francisco), **12, 13, 23**
San Francisco Chinatown dim sum
restaurants are generally open from
9 A.M. to 3 P.M. A few examples:
•❖Asia Gardens ☎415/398-5112
722 Pacific
•❖Golden Dragon ☎415/398-3920
822 Washington
•❖Louie's of Grant Ave.
☎415/982-5762
1014 Grant Ave.
•❖Hong Kong Tea House
835 Pacific Avenue
☎415/391-6365
Chinese New Year, **22** **date varies**
For information (San Francisco)
•❖San Francisco Visitor's Bureau
☎415/974-6900
•❖Chinese Chamber of Commerce
730 Sacramento Street
S. F. CA 94108 ☎415/982-3000
Chinese Spring Festival, **23**
☎415/986-1822
Christmas at Dunsmuir, **155, 171**
☎415/658-5019

F

Fall Festival (Aki Matsuri), **129**
☎415/922-6776
Fall Festival (Castro Valley), **129**
☎415/537-5300
Feast of Lanterns, **99**   ☎408/373-3304
Federal and legal holidays, **8**
Festival of the Sea, **71**   ☎415/771-3488
Fleet Week, **140**   ☎415/974-6900
Fisherman's Festival, **52**
☎707/875-3422
Fitzgerald Marine Reserve, **115**
☎415/728-3584
Folk Art International, **169**
☎415/673-4094
Folk Music Festival, **85**
☎415/441-5706
Fort Bragg, **72–73**. *See also* Mendocino
   Mendocino Coast Botanical
      Gardens   ☎707/964-4352
   •➔California Western Railway
      (Skunk Train)   ☎707/946-6371
      P.O. Box 907
      Fort Bragg, CA 95437
Fort Mason   ☎415/441-5705
Fort Ross, **101**   ☎707/865-2391
Fourth of July, **98**

G

Garlic Festival (Gilroy), **99**
☎408/842-1625
Gay Freedom Day Parade, **84**
☎415/974-6900
Golden Gate Dog Show, **23**
   tickets   ☎415/469-6000
Golden Gate Fields Wine Tasting
☎415/652-9202
Golden Gate Park, **118, 171**
   Asian Art Museum   ☎415/558-2993
   California Academy of Sciences
☎415/752-8268
   Morrison Planetarium
☎415/752-8268
   Conservatory of Flowers
☎415/558-3973
M.H. de Young Memorial Museum
☎415/558-2887
   Stow Lake   ☎415/752-0347
   Strybing Arboretum
☎415/661-1316
Golden Gate Park Band Shell, **85**
☎415/558-3706
Gold towns, **58-61**
Good Friday, **38**   **date varies**
Good Old Days Celebration, **53**
☎408/373-3304
Grand National Rodeo, **141**
☎415/469-6000
Grass Valley, **61**   ☎916/273-4667
Gray whale, **3,10**, **11**. *See also* Pacific
   gray whale
Great American Arts Festival, **98**
☎408/293-9727 or ☎408/998-7000
Greek festivals, **71, 141**
   Hayward (October)   ☎415/351-8292
   Oakland (May)   ☎415/531-7660
   San Jose (May)   ☎408/246-2700
   San Rafael (May)   ☎415/883-1998
Guerneville, **85, 129**

H

Hakone Japanese Gardens, **44**. *See also*
   Saratoga
Half Moon Bay, **70, 140, 142**
   •➔Chamber of Commerce
      P.O. Box 188
      Half Moon Bay, CA 94019
☎415/726-5202
   Art and Pumpkin Festival
☎415/726-5202
   Fitzgerald Marine Reserve
☎415/728-3584
Handel's *Messiah*, **169, 172**
   Check the December entertainment
   section of your newspaper for
   time and place of performance.
Handicraft Fair, **128**   ☎707/745-2120

Celebrations & Outings

Harvest Festival, **128, 154**
☎707/778-6300
Harvest Guides, **88–89**
The California Department of
Food and Agriculture will mail
you a free Farmer to Consumer
Directory based on counties.
Call toll free ☎800/952-5272
Please enclose large, self-addressed,
stamped envelope to:
•◆Alameda County Farm Trails
638 Enos Way
Livermore CA 94550
•◆Coastside Harvest Trails
(San Mateo County), Box 37
Half Moon Bay, CA 94019
•◆Contra Coast Harvest Time
P.O. Box O
Brentwood, CA 94513
•◆Country Crossroads
(Santa Clara & Santa Cruz Coun-
ties), 1368 North Fourth Street
San Jose, CA 95112
•◆Napa County Farm Trails
4075 Solano Avenue
Napa, CA 94558
•◆Sonoma County Farm Trails
Box 6674
Santa Rosa, CA 95406
•◆Yolano Harvest Trails
P.O. Box 484
Winters, CA 95694

Hayward, **110, 141**
Healdsburg, **39, 71, 129**
Holiday decorations, **171**
Holiday Faire-Christmas Lane, **155**
☎408/295-3050
Holleyberry Faire, **155**
☎707/433-6918
Hometown Days, **128** ☎415/593-1068

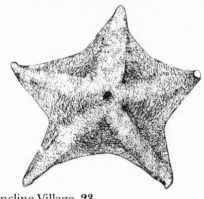

I

Ikebana Shows, **38**
Oakland ☎415/832-9329
San Francisco ☎415/752-0662

Incline Village, **23**
International Pumpkin Weigh-off and
Fair, **140, 142** ☎415/726-5202
Italian American Cultural
Festival, **140** ☎408/293-7122

J

Jack London State Park, **41**
☎707/938-5216
Jackson, **61**
Jamestown, **58**
Japan Center, **30, 53, 98**
information ☎415/922-6776
•◆Ginza Discount Imports
44 Peace Plaza ☎415/922-2475
•◆Kabuki Hot Springs
1750 Geary Boulevard
☎415/922-6000
•◆Kinokuniya Bookstore
1581 Webster ☎415/567-7625
•◆Soko Hardware
1698 Post ☎415/931-5510
Junior Grand National, **39**
☎415/469-6000

K

Kite Festival, **84** ☎415/974-6900
Klamath Basin National Wildlife
Refuge, **162**
KQED Wine and Food Festival, **154**
☎415/974-6900

L

Lafayette, Concours d'Elegance, **99**
Lake Tahoe, **39**, **116**. *See also* Snow, for
tourist organizations
•▸Emigrant Trail Museum
(Donner State Park)
☎916/587-3841
Inner tubing—rafting (Truckee
River)
Truckee River Raft Rentals
☎916/583-9724
Emerald Bay State Park
☎916/541-3030
D.L. Bliss State Park
☎916/525-7277
Desolation Wilderness
•▸U.S. Forest Service
P.O. Box 8465
South Lake Tahoe, CA 95705
Cruises (many more are available)
•▸Lake Tahoe Cruises
☎916/541-3364
M.S. Dixie Cruises
☎702/588-3508
Squaw Valley Tram
☎916/544-6263
Sand Harbor (Fine Arts Council)
☎916/546-5562
Virginia City Visitor's Bureau
☎702/847-0177
Lassen National Forest, **29**, **86–87**
For information write:
•▸Lassen National Forest
707 Nevada Street
Susanville, CA 96130
Lassen Volcanic National Park, **29**,
86–87   ☎916/595-4446
•▸Superintendent
Lassen Volcanic National Park
Mineral, CA 96063
For snowshoe trips   ☎916/595-4444
Lava Beds National Monument, **162**
☎916/667-2282
Los Gatos Cultural Festival, **110**
☎418/354-9300

M

Macy's Easter Flower Show, **38**
☎415/393-3017
Marin County Fair, **98**
☎415/499-6400
Marine life, **105**, **112–115**
McCloud dog sled races, **9**
☎916/964-2471
Mendocino, **72**. *See also* Fort Bragg
Mendocino Art Center
☎707/937-5818
Mendocino Park Information
☎707/937-5804
Mendocino—Fort Bragg Coast
•▸Chamber of Commerce
332 N. Main Street
P.O.Box 1141
Fort Bragg, CA 95437
☎707/964-3153
Kelly House Museum
☎707/937-5791
Menlo Town Fair, **84**   ☎415/325-2818
Midsummer Music Festival, **85**. *See also*
Stern Grove   ☎415/398-6551
Mill Valley, **70**, **84**, **111**
Mill Valley Film Festival, **111**
☎415/383-5256
Mill Valley Weekend, **70**
☎415/388-9700
Millbrae Arts and Wine Festival, **128**
☎415/697-7324
Mochi Pounding Ceremony, **169**
☎415/922-6776
Mokelumne Hill, **61**
Monarch butterfly, **160–161**
Mondavi Winery Music Festival, **85**
☎707/963-9611
Monterey, **42–43**
Monterey Bay Aquarium
☎408/375-3333
•▸Monterey Peninsula Visitors
Bureau, P.O. Box 1770
Monterey, CA 93940
☎408/649-3200

Monterey State Historic Park
☎408/649-2836
Monterey Jazz Festival, **129**
☎408/373-3366
Mt. Lassen, **86–87**. *See also* Lassen
Volcanic National Park
Mt. Tamalpais State Park, **62**
☎415/388-2070
Mud baths, **40**. *See also* Calistoga
Muir Woods National Monument, **57**
☎415/388-2595
Municipal Band Concerts (Oakland),
85   ☎415/839-9000
Murphys, **61**
Mushroom Fair, **9**   ☎415/342-7755
Music at Montalvo, **85**
☎408/867-3421 or ☎408/867-3586
Music at Paul Masson Winery, **71**
•❖P.O. Box 1852   ☎408/741-5181
Saratoga, CA 95070

N

Napa Town and Country Fair, **111**
☎707/224-7951
Napa Valley, **53**, **111**, **132**
•❖Beaulieu Vineyards
1960 St. Helena Highway
Rutherford, CA 94573
☎707/963-2411
•❖Beringer Vineyards
2000 Main Street
St. Helena, CA 94547
☎707/963-7115
•❖Calistoga Chamber of Commerce
1458 Lincoln Avenue
Calistoga, CA 94515
☎707/942-6333
•❖The Christian Brothers
Mt. LaSalle Vineyards
4111 Redwood Road
Napa, CA 94558   ☎707/226-5566

•❖The Christian Brothers
2555 Main Street
St. Helena, CA 94574
☎707/963-4480
•❖Domaine Chandon
California Drive
Yountville, CA 94599
☎707/944-2280
•❖Inglenook Vineyard Co.
1991 St. Helena Highway So.
Rutherford, CA 94573
☎707/963-7184
•❖Hanns Kornell Champagne
Cellars, 1091 Larkmead Lane
St. Helena, CA 94574
☎707/963-2334
•❖Charles Krug Winery
2800 Main Street
St. Helena, CA 94574
☎707/963-2761
•❖Louis M. Martini
P.O. Box 112   ☎707/963-2736
St. Helena Highway So.
St. Helena, CA 94575
•❖Robert Mondavi Winery
7801 St. Helena Highway
Oakville, CA 94562
☎707/963-9611
•❖The Oakville Grocery
7856 St. Helena Highway
Oakville, CA 94562
☎707/944-8802
•❖Old Bale Grist-Mill State
Historic Park   ☎707/942-4575
3801 St. Helena Highway
Calistoga, CA 94515
•❖St. Helena Chamber of Com-
merce, 1508 Main Street
(P.O. Box 124)
St. Helena, CA 94574
☎707/963-4456
•❖Sterling Vineyards☎707/942-5151
1111 Dunaweal Lane
Calistoga, CA 94515
•❖Vintage 1870   ☎707/944-2451
6525 Washington Street
Yountville, CA 94599

National Begonia Festival, **129**
Nevada City, **61, 145**
•❖Chamber of Commerce
132 Main Street ☎916/265-2692
Nevada City, CA 95959
•❖The National Hotel
211 Broad Street ☎916/265-4551
•❖Red Castle
109 Prospect Street
☎916/265-5135
•❖Kenton Mine Lodge and Cookhouse, P.O. Box 942
Alleghany CA 95910
☎916/287-3212
Nevada Theater ☎916/265-6161
Firehouse Museum
☎916/265-9941
American Victorian Museum
☎916/265-5804
Nikkei Matsuri, **39** ☎408/297-8516
North Beach Fair, **84** ☎415/346-4446
North Beach Photo Fair, **70**
☎415/974-6900
Novato, **85, 110**
Nutcracker ballet, **169, 173**
San Francisco Ballet
☎415/621-3838
Oakland Ballet ☎415/465-640C
Peninsula Ballet ☎415/343-8485
Berkeley Conservatory Ballet
☎415/642-9988 or 841-8913
Marin Civic Ballet ☎415/472-3500
San Jose Dance Theater
☎408/298-2302 or 371-9561

O

Oakland, **6, 23, 52, 85, 140, 155, 169**
Obon Festival, **99** ☎408/293-9292
Occidental, **101**. *See also* Russian River
Octoberfest, **141**
Lake Tahoe Octoberfest
☎916/583-2371
Old Adobe Fiesta, **111** ☎707/762-2785

Old Time Fiddlers Contest, **9**
☎707/894-5790 or 894-2067
Old Sacramento, **144**
•❖Visitors Bureau ☎916/449-5291
1100 14th Street
Sacramento, CA 95814
•❖California State Railroad
Museum, Second and I Streets
Old Sacramento, CA 95814
☎916/445-7373
•❖Sutter's Fort
2701 L. Street
Sacramento ☎916/445-4209
Orchid Show, **38** ☎415/558-3622
Opening day of the yachting season,
53 ☎415/469-6065
Oysters, **37, 124, 130, 166**. *See also*
the Ready Reference—Foods (oysters) for the locations of oyster beds.

P

Pacific Coast iris, **45**
Pacific gray whale, **3, 10, 11**
for information and whale trips:
•❖Whale Center
3929 Piedmont Avenue
Oakland, CA 94611
☎415/ 654-6691
•❖Oceanic Society
San Francisco Bay Chapter
Building E, Fort Mason
San Francisco, CA 94123
☎415/474-6767
These museums often feature
special exhibits and lectures:
Point Reyes ☎415/663-1093
Lawrence Hall of Science
(Berkeley) ☎415/642-5132
Coyote Point ☎415/342-7755

Celebrations & Outings

For information on Point Reyes:
●◆Point Reyes National Seashore
Point Reyes, CA 94956
☎415/663-1092
For information on Monterey
fishing (observation) cruises:
Visitor's Bureau ☎408/649-3200
Pacific Grove, **53, 99, 160**
●◆Chamber of Commerce
P.O. Box 167
Pacific Grove, CA 93950
☎408/373-3304
●◆Museum of Natural History
165 Forest Avenue ☎408/372-4212
Pacific Grove, CA 93950
Point Pinos Lighthouse
☎408/373-3304
●◆Asilomar Conference Center
P.O. Box 537 ☎408/372-8016
Pacific Grove, CA 93950
Pacific States Crafts Fair, **110**
☎415/441-5705
Pacifica Fog Fest, **128** ☎415/355-4122
Palo Alto, **9**
Pan Pacific Exposition Festival, **128**
☎415/974-6900
Paul Masson Mountain Winery
Concerts, **71** ☎408/725-4275
●◆P.O. Box 1852
Saratoga, CA 95070
Paul Masson vineyards, **44**. *See also*
Saratoga
Peach Blossom Festival, **23**
☎415/960-4302
Peddler's Fair, **110** ☎707/745-2120
Piedmont, **140**
Placerville, **61** ☎916/622-5611
Point Reyes National Seashore, **11,
130–131**
Visitor's Center (Drake's Beach)
☎415/669-1250
Lighthouse ☎415/669-1534
Youth hostel ☎415/669-9985
Park camping ☎415/663-1092
For oyster beds see Oysters in the
Ready Reference—Foods (oys-
ters)

Polk St. Art Fair, **99** ☎415/974-6900
Potter's show and sale, **155**
☎415/974-6900
Pumpkins, **135, 140, 142, 143**
●◆The Nut Tree (Great Scarecrow
Competition) ☎707/448-1818
located at the junction of highways 80 and 505, 1½ miles east
of Vacaville
●◆Great Whitehall Lane Pumpkin
Patch, 1285 Whitehall Lane
St. Helena, CA 94574
☎707/963-4914
●◆John Spina Farms (pumpkins)
several locations in San Jose
●◆pumpkins are sold in many locations at Half Moon Bay
☎415/726-5202

R

Redwood Empire Jazz Festival, **155**
☎707/664-2712
Redwoods, **54–57**
Renaissance Pleasure Faire, **110**
☎415/892-2166
Rhododendrons, **52**
Roaring Camp & Big Trees Railroad,
57 ☎408/335-4484
Rodeos, **39, 53, 99, 141**
Rose pruning demonstrations, **9**
Oakland ☎415/273-3090
San Francisco ☎415/558-4268
Russian River, **71, 100–101, 129**
●◆Visitor's Center ☎707/869-9009
P.O. Box 255
Guerneville, CA 95446

canoe rentals ☎707/433-7247
c/o Trowbridge Recreation Inc.
20 Healdsburg Avenue
Healdsburg, CA 95448
Occidental Italian restaurants
Fiori's ☎707/823-8188
Negri's ☎707/823-5301
Union Hotel ☎707/874-3662
Fort Ross State Historic Park
☎707/847-3286
Russian River Country Music
Festival, **85** ☎707/869-9009
Russian River Jazz Festival, **129**
☎707/887-1502
Russian River Wine Festival, **71**
☎707/869-9009

S

Sacramento, **39, 70, 111, 144**
Saint Patrick's Day, **38** **March 17**
Oakland parade ☎415/839-9000
San Francisco parade
☎415/562-8136
Sacramento parade
☎916/442-5542
snake race ☎415/392-4880
Salinas, **99**
Samuel P. Taylor Park, **57**
☎415/488-9897
San Andreas, **61**
San Anselmo County Fair Day, **128**
☎415/454-2510
San Bruno, **140**
San Francisco, **9, 12, 23, 30, 38, 39,
52, 53, 70, 71, 84, 85, 98, 99, 110,
118, 129, 140, 154, 155, 168, 169,
171, 172, 173**
San Francisco Art Festival, **84**
☎415/558-3463 or 558-4888

San Francisco Blues Festival, **129**
☎415/441-5706
San Francisco Fair, **98**
☎415/557-8758
San Francisco Landscape Garden
Show, **52** ☎415/974-6900
San Francisco Summer Festival, **85**
☎415/974-6900
San Jose, **39, 71, 98, 99, 111, 128, 129,
140, 155, 169**
San Jose Harvest Festival, **128**
☎408/998-7000
San Mateo, **110**
San Rafael, **98, 140, 169**
Santa Clara County Fair, **111**
☎408/295-3050
Santa Clara Festival Days, **140**
☎408/246-9190
Santa Cruz, **23, 90**. *See also* Capitola
Santa Cruz County Visitor's Bu-
reau P.O. Box 921
Santa Cruz, CA 95061
☎408/423-1111
Boardwalk ☎408/423-5590
(Located at Beach Street and
Riverside Avenue)
P.O. Box 625
Santa Cruz 95061
Natural Bridges State Beach
☎408/423-4609
New Brighton State Beach
☎408/475-4870
Sunset State Beach ☎408/724-1266

Santa Rosa, **129, 141**
Saratoga, **44, 71, 85**
Saratoga Chamber of Commerce
P.O. Box 161 ☎408/867-0753
Saratoga, CA 95070
Villa Montalvo Center for the
Arts (Off Highway 9)
P.O. Box 158 ☎408/867-3586
Saratoga, CA 95071
Paul Masson Vineyards
13150 Saratoga Avenue
Saratoga, CA 95071
☎408/257-7800

➤Hakone Japanese Gardens
located just outside Saratoga
on Big Basin Way ☎408/867-3438
Saratoga Rotary Arts and Crafts
Festival, **70** ☎408/867-0753
Sausalito, **14,128**
➤The Bay Model
2100 Bridgeway ☎415/332-3970
Sausalito Art Festival, **128**
☎415/332-0505
Scottish Gathering and Games, **128**
☎707/545-1414
Sea otter, **33, 43**. *See also* California
sea otter
Seals, **15, 24–27**
Sequoia and Kings Canyon National
Parks, **29** ☎209/565-3341
➤Hospitality Service
Sequoia National Park, CA 93262
Shore birds, **149, 157–159, 162**
Singing Christmas Tree, **169**
San Jose ☎408/246-6790
San Rafael ☎415/479-1360
Skiing, **28**
Skunk train, **73**. *See also* Fort Bragg
☎707/964-3061
Snow, **28–29**
➤Tahoe North Visitors Bureau
P.O. Box 5578 ☎916/583-3494
Tahoe City, CA 95730
➤South Tahoe Visitor Bureau
P.O. Box 177727 ☎916/544-5050
South Lake Tahoe, CA 95706
Snowfest, **39** ☎916/583-2371
Sonoma Coast, **156**
Bodega Dunes ☎707/875-3483
Wrights Beach ☎707/875-3483
Sonoma County Harvest Fair, **141**
☎707/545-4200
Sonora, **58** ☎209/532-4212
Spring Blossom Festival, **39**
☎707/433-6935

Spring Folk Music Festival, **85**
☎415/441-5706
Spring wildflowers, **45, 55, 56, 59, 60**
Stellar sea lion, **26**

Stern Grove, **85**
➤Festival Association
P.O. Box 3250
San Francisco, CA 94119
☎415/398-6551
➤picnic table reservations
☎415/558-4728
St. Helena, **110**
Stinson Beach, **112**
➤weather conditions
☎415/868-1922
St. Patrick's Day, **38** **March 17**
See Saint Patrick's Day
Strybing Arboretum, **174**
Summer Music Festival, **85**
☎707/963-9611
Summer Solstice, **84** **about June 22**
Sunny Hills Grape Festival, **140**
☎415/454-4163
Sunnyvale Arts and Wine Festival, **84**
☎408/736-4971

T

Tanabata (star festival), **98**
☎415/922-6776
Tidal pool life, **115**
Ticketron, Inc. ☎415/393-6914

Tilden Regional Park, **104**
➤ East Bay Regional Park District
11500 Skyline Boulevard
Oakland, CA 94619
☎415/531-9330
Tilden Park office ☎415/843-2137

Environmental Education Center
☎415/525-2233
Tomales Bay State Park, **130**. *See also*
Point Reyes ☎415/669-1140
Truckee, **23** ☎415/273-3090
Tsu Kimi, **141**

U

Union Street Spring Festival, **84**
☎415/421-5074
University of California and Stanford
football game (Big Game), **155**
Upper Grant Avenue Street Fair, **84**
☎415/421-5074

V

Vernal equinox, **38**
approximately **March 21**
Victorian Days, **110** ☎415/574-6441
Villa Montalvo Center for the
Arts, **44**, **85**.
(located off Highway 9)
➤ P.O. Box 158
Saratoga, CA 95071
☎408/867-3586
Violet, title page, **56**
Volcano, **61**

W

Weather (Bay Area), **1**, **31**, **77**, **119**,
147
Weather Service ☎415/936-1212
Whale, **3**, **10–11**. *See also* Pacific gray
whale
Wildflowers, **45**, **54–61**
Wine Festival, **84** ☎408/388-9700
Wineries, **125**, **132–133**. *See also* Napa
Valley and the Ready Reference—
Foods (Wineries, Bay Area)
Winter solstice about **December 22**
Winterskol, (Incline Village), **23**
☎702/831-1433

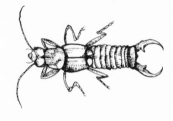

Y

Yosemite, **29**, **74–75**
➤ Superintendent
P.O. Box 577
Yosemite National Park, CA 95389
for reservations
➤ Yosemite Park and Curry Co.
Yosemite National Park, CA 95389
☎209/373-4171
Yuletide at Montalvo, **168**
☎408/867-3586

About the Author

Katherine Grace Endicott is the gardening columnist for the *San Francisco Chronicle*. She won a 1988 Quill and Trowel Communication Award by the Garden Writers' Association of America in recognition of significant achievement and high standards of excellence. She grows most of the plants discussed in the gardening sections of *Seasonal Expectations*, as well as many of the vegetables, herbs, and berries discussed in the food sections.

OTHER TIOGA BOOKS YOU WILL ENJOY

Garden Getaways: Northern California

Nona Pierce

Over 100 public gardens and special nurseries within two hours of San Francisco are described. Entries include the ambiance, special plants, directions, facilities, handicap access.

176 pages. Black-white photos. Softcover. $12.95

Making the Most of the Peninsula

Lee Foster

A well-researched and comprehensive guide to San Mateo, Santa Clara, and Santa Cruz counties. Includes cultural and natural history, architecture, hikes, excursions.

290 pages. Black-white photos. Softcover. $11.95

San Francisco Bay Area Landmarks: Reflections of Four Centuries

Charles Kennard. Foreword by James D. Houston

Handsome duotone photographs, historical quotations, and modern commentary bring alive the stories of the land and people around the Golden Gate.

160 pages. Hardcover. $35.00

TO ORDER

Send a check including applicable sales tax and $1.50 for the first book; $.50 each additional to cover postage and handling to:

Tioga Publishing Company
Box 50490
Palo Alto CA 94303